WORKING AN INTEGRATED DAY

I. Allen, K. Douet, M. Gaff, E. Gray,
C. Griffiths, N. Ryall, E. Toone

Ward Lock Educational

ISBN 0 7062 3454 5 hardback
0 7062 3455 3 paperback

First published 1975

Set in 11 on 12 point Monotype Baskerville
and printed by Robert MacLehose and Company Limited, Glasgow
for Ward Lock Educational
116 Baker Street, London W1M 2BR
Made in Great Britain

CONTENTS

DEDICATION

The members of the group wish to dedicate this book to the many teachers with whom they became associated during the survey period. We should like to take this opportunity of thanking them all for their help during observations and discussions and for their comments on the manuscript as it was being prepared. In particular we should wish to make special acknowledgment of the help received from:

Mrs J. Le Masurier, formerly Senior Lecturer, St Katherines College of Education, Liverpool

Mrs P. Iliffe, Head of Uplands Infant School, Leicester

Miss N. B. Bloor, formerly Head of Overdale Infant School, Leicester

Mrs L. Dickens, Head of Queensmead Infant School, Leicester

We are grateful to headteachers who have welcomed us to their schools and who have kindly given their evenings to come and talk to us and discuss problems. We are also indebted to those headteachers who have released staff to observe the work of other schools and bring back information to the group.

The School of Education of the University of Leicester was most cooperative during the two years of our survey and we are grateful for their hospitality throughout the writing of this book.

Leicester, April 1975

PREFACE

On the invitation of the School of Education, University of Leicester, a group of teachers from local schools met to discuss the interpretation of the term 'integrated day' and to study the various ways in which it was actually implemented in schools for young children. Throughout the ensuing year these teachers visited nursery, infant and junior schools, in both the city and country, and their visits were followed by discussion groups, often with the headteachers of the schools concerned. Thus the teachers who had visited a school during the day were able to give an account of their visit to the whole group at a meeting that evening and the headteachers were asked to add their own comments and to answer questions. During the first year visits were made to schools using an integrated day organization and particular note was taken of the type of building and of the facilities available, as well as the different ways of implementing the idea of the integrated day.

Subsequently it was decided that a subcommittee should begin to write up the notes of these visits with a view to publication as it was generally felt that there was insufficient reference material available for teachers on how the integrated day is working out in practice. The group hoped that a publication of this nature would be particularly helpful to young teachers, many of whom have not had the opportunity of teaching in integrated day schools during their college courses and encounter great difficulties in trying to organize their classes in this way on first appointment. So this book mainly contains practical suggestions and definite information about work and class structures and organization. Mature teachers may find some of this material relevant to their own problems, particularly if they are endeavouring to change to this type of programme. We hope that it will also be useful to heads who are thinking of changing the organization of their schools.

Once the outline of the proposed publication had been discussed, the character of the school visits changed to enable the observers to visit schools for more specific data. The nature of the observations for the second year encompassed material needed by the sub-committee and the group visited schools where they could observe vertical and transitional grouping, the teaching of immigrant children and parental involvement with schools. Additionally, observations were made on reading, mathematics, music, science and field study work. As in the previous year, the group making visits to schools reported to the central group at regular evening meetings. In this way all the work of writing has resulted from group observations and discussions, which have been used throughout for the basis of this book. All illustrative material is reported from real people, places and situations; only the names are fictitious.

INTRODUCTION

The term 'integrated day' means, in effect, the freeing of the school from an organized timetable apart from such periods as affect the whole community, such as assemblies, hall periods, and periods where classes combine and make timetabling essential. The integrated day encourages flexibility in ways of teaching and of learning, to the advantage and satisfaction of both teacher and child.

On an empirical basis, it appeared to us that the philosophy behind the integrated day is that by this freedom children are enabled to derive the maximum benefit from every resource at their disposal, and from every discovery which they are encouraged to make, guided by those who teach them. However, it is generally accepted that freedom in this sense must never be confused with licence to employ their time exactly as they wish. Disciplines are necessary if the children are to gain a basically acceptable standard of education; but within the framework of the integrated day, which permits them ample opportunity to develop their interests, such disciplines are in the main accepted. Teachers felt that most children understand that there is certain work which they are expected to undertake, and to which they will be expected to devote a reasonable amount of their time, that these tasks are considered by their teachers to be both important and desirable and that teachers, on their part, will present them as attractively as possible.

The flexibility of the integrated day gives teachers a chance to stretch the children to their full capacity and at the same time provides for their development as personalities within various social groups. There is more chance for development without the anxieties of being expected to submit to undue pressures or to a feeling that they may fail or be left behind. The pressure is applied only by the children themselves.

The teacher who is willing to work an integrated day may find that she has gained much from the experience. Her personal knowledge of and contact with the children will be increased by increased opportunity for free communication and the varied activities of her school day will help her to extend her own horizons. The anticipatory sense of discovery which emanates from a well-run integrated day situation is a very effective safeguard against monotony and the consequent waning of enthusiasm. The achievements and progress made should give the teacher added satisfaction, for they will have come about with the active cooperation of the children.

Chapter 1

GROUPING AND PLANNING

Grouping

Schools that work an integrated day are often led by this challenge to reconsider the way in which the pupils are organized into classes or groups. The Plowden Report states:

> Most primary school work is done in classes. The children who form a class spend most of the day with their class teacher. This is what teachers are used to and what overwhelmingly they think right. More than two thirds of those in our sample of primary school teachers thought that the class teacher should be mainly responsible for his class, while *a further quarter accepted the system but thought that the class teacher could reasonably share more of his responsibilities with other teachers.*

More flexible methods of teaching mean that teachers begin to question and adapt the traditional methods of allocating children to groups and often feel the need to cooperate with other teachers or take advantage of a colleague's particular skills. If a school wishes to change from formal teaching to working within an integrated day, one of the first considerations is whether a new system of grouping might be beneficial for the children and the teachers.

Historically, chronological and vertical grouping were the usual ways of grouping children, and are still retained in this country as the main methods of organizing children in schools. Vertical grouping, originating in small country schools, has been increasingly adopted by larger town schools, and within the last decade schools have also experimented with transitional grouping as a compromise between the two original forms but with its own rationale.

Chronological grouping

By chronological grouping we mean complete classes of the same age. In large schools, with three or four parallel classes in each year, this may mean only a three-month age range within each class. On the other hand, in a small school there will be a much wider age range — anything up to one year.

The advantages of chronological grouping

1 Teachers may feel more secure with a narrow age range. Their task seems simpler as the range of ability appears to be less than in classes where children are vertically grouped.
2 With each school year, both children and teachers can make a completely fresh start putting past mistakes and failures behind them.
3 It is often thought that chronologically-grouped classes display greater social cohesion and interaction since the children tend to be at the same level of socio-emotional development and have similar levels of interest.

The disadvantages of chronological grouping

1 At the beginning of the school year the whole class is new, with no nucleus of children left over from the previous year to continue class tradition or routine.
2 In the last year of the infant school, where there are parallel classes with narrowly differentiated age ranges, too many children who need help in reading may be concentrated in the youngest seven year old class.
3 The children in the younger parallel classes may do less well, even when allowance is made for their age, because they are known to be younger and appear less able. The teacher expects less from them so they tend to underachieve.
4 Teachers may be persuaded that they have a homogeneous class, all at much the same level, and be blinded to the exceptions. For example, it is fairly common to find in a class of seven year olds that reading ages vary between five and eleven or twelve years; some children will have barely made a start while others will be fluent readers. In the same way, some seven year olds still have a very tenuous grasp of the most basic number concepts while others are able to work out complicated number relationships and often relate their knowledge of computation to environmental studies. Remarks of children such as, 'My father says that 25 is $\frac{1}{4}$ of 100 and I've been thinking then $12\frac{1}{2}$ is $\frac{1}{8}$ of 100, isn't it?' and 'My sister is eleven and I'm seven, so when I'm eleven, she'll be fifteen, won't she?'

are typical of this kind of mathematical grasp, but their significance can well be missed by teachers who are thinking in terms of 'a seven-year old class'.

5 Many teachers tend to specialize in one age group for several or even many years, becoming known as a 'reception class teacher', or 'a top infant teacher'. This may considerably narrow the range of a teacher's experience.

6 A small school where there is an intake each term means that a child may spend only one term in the reception class and subsequently very short periods in any of the other classes due to pressure of new entrants.

Vertical grouping

By vertical grouping we mean that groups from each new intake of children are successively distributed into each class, until the entire age-compass of the school is to be found in every classroom. In the average infant school using this method of grouping, one would expect to find five, six and seven year olds represented by small units in each classroom, and attached to the teacher of each class.

The advantages of vertical grouping

1 There is no difficulty in placing a newcomer into a class, as he will find children of his own age group and mentality in whichever room is chosen and he will also have the company of children of different ages.

2 Should there be any 'personality' clashes — between child and teacher or child and child — or a lack of progression on the part of the child, he can be moved to another class without difficulty.

3 Vertical grouping gives an atmosphere of stability and removes the awkward situation which sometimes arises with chronological grouping in which a child may spend as little as one term in his first two classes — a very unsettling experience.

4 Within the vertical grouping situation, the child has the chance to become familiar with his surroundings for a sustained period of time.

5 The presence of mixed age groups gives greater opportunities for different levels of conversation and speech. The atmosphere is more that of the natural family, and the child is therefore less inhibited.

6 The older children acquire a sense of responsibility towards the younger ones.

7 The problems of the various age groups are experienced by every teacher in the vertical grouping situation, thus establishing a common denominator for discussion and exchange of ideas and experiences.

8 Under this system, the numbers in each class are evened out.

9 In the vertically-grouped class, there is not such a break in the teaching of basic skills.

10 As the children become more stable, the teacher is able to know and understand them better.

11 Within the framework of the vertically-grouped situation, the children are able to find their own level. The slower child, for example, may work with a younger group without attracting awkward attention. In fact the children find their emotional and mental level and are able to work within it.

12 Teachers using vertical grouping speak favourably of it, and are very aware of its advantages.

The disadvantages of vertical grouping

1 One of the chief problems appears to be a misunderstanding on the part of parents who believe, however misguidedly, that by staying a further year in the same class their children are being victimized in some way, despite evidence to the contrary; or they may fail to understand the advantages to their children in being educated with other age groups, and feel these groups in some way impede their children's progress.

2 There may be a tendency for the older children to help the younger ones too much, thus impeding their own progress. Nor should the older child be permitted to become a kind of teacher-substitute.

3 It is sometimes difficult to preserve equal opportunities for each age group in the class, for example the needs of the seven year olds may be given undue stress just because their elevation to the junior school is imminent.

4 Unless teachers make comparisons of work right through the school at each age level, so that they cross-reference the standards of each age in every other class, children of equal age and ability may leave the school with unnecessarily different attainments. Headteachers in some schools ask all teachers to hand in each month the work of the seven, or six year olds in their classes, so that both the head and the teachers can see that a comparable standard is being kept throughout the school. Failure to seek such comparisons may impair

teachers' efficiency and be contrary to the best interests of the children.

5 It is difficult to cater for the physical and mental capabilities of the various age groups in certain subjects and it would be advisable to group the children into ages, drawing on more than one class, for such activities as PE, story time, music and movement, where skill is largely dependent on maturation.

6 Where there is a changeover to single-age classes at junior school level a certain amount of unsettled feeling may arise in some children accustomed to working in groups, though we feel that at seven plus years, many would appreciate it.

7 Children who are in the care of weak, uninterested or supply teachers are seriously disadvantaged by vertical grouping, and many of the objectives of vertical grouping have to be abandoned if such teachers have to be given a different class each year. Desperate parents have been known to complain that their children have not had an adequate teacher by the age of nine years, after four years of schooling.

The advantages of vertical grouping seem on balance to outweigh the disadvantages, and we feel as a group that this system could be a very positive advantage in schools with a large number of immigrant children or in deprived areas, where the sense of security matters a great deal, and also where the 'family' situation, probably already existing at home, can be equated with the 'family' atmosphere of school classroom.

Finally, the teachers who work in vertically-grouped schools must obviously liaise closely with each other and have faith in the system if the maximum benefit is to be derived from it.

Transitional grouping

Within this system, in the infant school one would expect to find the five and six year olds vertically-grouped together in parallel classes, proceeding to single-age classes for those who are seven, though in certain schools this arrangement is very flexible. In the 'first school', we mainly found that the fives and sixes were vertically-grouped and then proceeded to further vertical-grouped classes containing the seven and eight year olds.

The rationale for transitional grouping seems largely to depend on a recognition of the considerable intellectual and social development which is particularly noticeable between six and seven. The younger child is largely engaged in the formation of concepts relative to physical and social reality, in learning to separate fact from phantasy and desire. He tends to be adult-orientated and to regard the peer group as rivals.

By seven or eight, the child is normally engaged in learning to manipulate fact, in acquiring skills and the concepts essential to everyday life. He is learning to be peer-group related and to adopt the appropriate personal and sex role within the group. It is now becoming highly important to behave as the others behave, to wear what they wear and to have parents who conform to the group's expectations of parental behaviour, whereas earlier the opinion or ability of the adult was the criterion, shown in such statements as, 'My Dad is bigger than yours', 'My Mum says', or 'Teacher says'. Seven year old boys are increasingly concerned to behave like boys, to do the masculine things, to avoid being 'cissy', whereas girls are beginning to distinguish and adopt the current feminine role.

It is often difficult to provide for both sevens and fives in one class since they find communication difficult. The sevens may regard the phantasy of the fives as 'silly' and the fives may find the practical sevens incomprehensible. An example of this pattern arose when a seven year old boy was discussing how his bicycle works with a five year old. 'You see, the chain goes round the little wheel and then round the hub of the big wheel and that makes the big wheel go faster than the small wheel.' 'They're both wheels,' said the five year old, 'they go round.' 'Oh, you're silly,' said the seven year old and walked off. 'I'm an ambulance,' said the five year old, and rode away making siren noises.

Advantages of transitional grouping

1 While there is stability for newcomers (as with vertical grouping) and the children will not be 'pushed up' a class to make room for a new intake as may happen with chronological grouping, with transitional grouping children have the experience of making a break within the security of their first school. Headteachers often expressed the opinion that if the children stayed too long with one teacher, they tended to find adjustment at the junior or middle school level very difficult.

2 For children to spend the whole of their first school life with one teacher may be to distribute most unfairly the interests, abilities and weaknesses of the teaching staff. Transitional grouping allows the children more variety of adult contact while giving the head a chance to balance the strengths of the

teachers who are successively responsible for a class of children. This does not only mean that weak teachers should be followed by adequate teachers, but that other kinds of contrasting skills may be deployed for the children's benefit. For instance a practical teacher may be followed by an imaginative teacher, a teacher whose skills are mainly scientific or mathematical may be succeeded by one who is mainly arts-centred or even a sports enthusiast.

3 Separating the children at seven appeared to eliminate the need to cater for PE, story and music at a separate level for certain ages as within the vertically-grouped class.

4 Transitional grouping appeared to help with the problem of the younger children trying to follow too closely the lead of the older children, and loosing experience of activities such as phantasy play or the investigation of the properties of materials. The older children in separate classes can expect more opportunity to use materials creatively and more teacher's help with the practice of the basic skills which normally require daily attention.

5 A financial advantage of transitional grouping is that apparatus may be bought for either the younger or older age group. This can be an expensive item in a large school organized only for vertical grouping.

6 Some teachers are definitely happier teaching older chiluren, and others are more suited to the very young. The separation of transitional grouping can lead to a more fertile climate at both levels.

7 Although in theory the idea of 'family' as suggested by vertical grouping is desirable, in practice this is not necessarily so. An older child in a large family at home, who may possibly be expected to care for the younger ones out of school hours, may well be resentful of the ties imposed by such a situation at school and welcome the breakaway from such responsibilities. It is possible within the framework of the transitionally-grouped school to allow a child sufficient access to a younger or older child to enable that child to settle down without imposing undue responsibility and strain.

In the socially-deprived school, we found that this system appeared to have much to offer, providing a stable atmosphere, mental and social stimulation and favourable conditions for speech and language development suitable to the child's level.

Disadvantages of transitional grouping

1 Where an individual child has not emotionally or intellectually reached the level of his companions, this is obviously more noticeable on transfer to a seven year old class or vertically-grouped seven to eight year class. One can only hope for the kind of flexibility which will best enable such an individual to find his true level without becoming alienated from his own age group, mainly by building on his strengths rather than emphasizing, or allowing the children to emphasize, his weaknesses.

2 As with vertical grouping, there may well be misunderstandings by the parents which need sympathetic explanation by the school.

3 Where children have made friends with older or younger children in their vertically-grouped class and are now separated, there may be real distress on the part of the children and the parents which should be understood by the school; and as it may well be a recurrent situation throughout school life, relevant insight may be needed. The child who moves on to the older class has the excitement of novelty but the child who is left behind may well have no friend in the class and may need to be helped to find one.

Team teaching

In the 'first school' we found that the demands made on the teacher in providing adequately for vertically-grouped classes of seven and eight year olds were such that some form of teacher exchange, cooperation, or skill sharing became absolutely essential. No single individual could cope with the variety of needs and interests of some children at this level. Team teaching was adopted in many schools as an answer to this problem and as a means of making the skills of each teacher available to a wide range of children.

Team teaching is a further development of working an integrated day, whereby a team of teachers shares the overall education of a large number of children. A team may be formed by only two teachers with accompanying children or by any number up to six, possibly including the whole staff. The size of the team is often related to the layout of building, and also to the compatability of the teachers.

Each teacher may then take responsibility for a particular facet of education, i.e. mathematics, language, art and craft, and rooms will be used for only one or two activities. In some schools the teachers may not wish to teach only one 'subject'. Here the teachers may change their activities fairly frequently. Periods of two up to eight weeks were suggested in a specific teaching area. In these circumstances it would be necessary to have one teacher with overall responsibility for each subject and so, when a teacher begins a period in charge of, for example, mathematics, she would discuss the children's problems and further development with both her predecessor in the room and the specialist.

A team may consist of all the children of one age group in a school, or it may be vertically-grouped as would be the case if the whole school formed one team. Experience has shown that the reception class children benefit from a term on their own to establish themselves securely in school, though where there is a nursery class this is not as necessary.

Cooperation between teachers is essential in team teaching and there needs to be constant contact and discussion. Careful records are most important.

The children, though they move freely from one work area to another, need to have a base in a particular room where they can keep their possessions and a particular teacher to call their own.

The economic advantages of team teaching are great; since all the equipment for a particular activity will be in one room, much duplication will be avoided. It is often possible to purchase larger and more expensive apparatus as a result. Economy of time is of even greater value, since whilst a teacher is only involved in one activity at a time, she is able to range widely within that activity and to explore each child's potential in it to a greater depth. Thus she is able to give all the children the opportunity to work to their limits which is not always possible in a classroom of many varied activities.

The organization of team teaching

Each teacher will have a register of the children to whom she acts as guardian, and these children will go to her on arrival each day in the same room for registration and a quick exchange of news. This daily contact is important.

For the daily working of the team there must be a brief assembly of all members so that children are told of the activities in which they are expected to participate during the day, and each teacher can then explain any new or special activity going on in her room. This is obviously not a teaching but more a 'catching of interest' time. The children then disperse to the activity of their choice and this is an opportune time to take out any groups for a specific purpose.

For example, the teaching of reading in such a team situation might be organized as follows. In a large team, one room may be set aside for reading, with a carpeted area, comfortable chairs and attractive books as a library corner, another section for phonic and word work and a teacher to hear reading. In a smaller team the same apparatus can be fitted in with writing, though the teachers in the other rooms must help with the reading in their spare moments. A record card clipped in each book, with pages reached written in different coloured pens for each day is a quick check. Phonic problems should be reported to the teacher in charge. She should also change all reading books thus keeping a check on each child's progress. The teaching of mathematics would be organized in a similar way.

PE, TV, music, story, dance

Groups can be taken out of the team for these activities. It may be possible for the whole team to lay down tools and go to another activity at the same time. Alternatively it may be necessary for a room to be closed for a period whilst the teacher takes a group for one of these activities.

In some schools we have seen the PE apparatus erected on alternate mornings when the head or a part-time teacher could be spared to supervise and the children then go at will, using a simple system of hanging name tags on hooks so that the apparatus is not overloaded and everyone has a fair turn.

Problem children

Behaviour problems usually arise from various forms of basic insecurity and these children cannot cope with the same freedom as others without more help and experience. A solution for them is to establish a routine, for example they report in the mathematics area first in the morning, for language work after play and for art and craft or science in the afternoon. They then gain the security of a definite form of procedure so that both they and the teachers know where they should be, until they have matured sufficiently to be able to manage more freedom of choice.

How to begin

To embark on team teaching needs many weeks of careful thought and preparation. It must be well-organized from the beginning and even so the first few weeks will seem chaotic. At the start it is hard work, but gradually problems are ironed out and by the second term it is usually working well and the benefits begin to show. An interesting point is that the children may settle into the situation more easily than the teachers.

We feel it is wise to begin slowly with one team, perhaps just a combination of two classes, so that schools may feel their way. In any event we gained the impression that a three-class team with up to 120 children is the optimum from the point of view of the children, except where a school is purpose-built to be worked in by one team.

Although this is true of all learning situations, training in self-discipline is particularly important in team teaching, so that children learn to use their time wisely, without a great amount of fuss or adult supervision. Under any form of organization there will be children who are inclined to drift, to take the easy way out, to demand undue attention. Team teaching gives these children opportunities for time-frittering unless the teachers are thoroughly aware and take appropriate steps. But teachers experienced in team work are sure that average children will prosper both in their work and in their social progress and they will achieve a high standard of self-reliance, self-discipline and good sense.

However desirable the introduction of team teaching may be, the layout of the buildings is of primary importance and to introduce a large team in an unsuitable building with too much corridor and passage space between rooms is to court disaster. Additionally each teaching area must be suitably equipped to cater for the differing ages and levels of attainment of the children. If carefully planned this can be an economical way of equipping the teaching areas.

Planning

The second factor that must be considered before introducing an integrated day is the kind of day that each teacher feels she is able to organize and run successfully. Not every teacher in a school must have the same kind of integrated day, in fact there are possibly as many kinds of integrated day as there are teachers. However, there seem to be two basic ways of planning an integrated day on which teachers build their own individual interpretations.

1 *Organized groups*

Groups of children are directed to specific work areas for a stated length of time and then move on to another activity. For example, a group starts off in the morning in the painting area, and goes on during the course of the day to the reading area (in the book corner), the writing area (with access to dictionaries or, in the case of younger children, to various writing and tracing materials), the word games and reading apparatus area, and the mathematics or science area. The social areas, which usually have to be used by limited numbers of children at one time, can be incorporated into any one of these areas depending on the subject of the social area that day. This method does provide a time for hearing children read each day since each group which comes to the reading area has a chance to read to the teacher. The teacher arranges the plan of the day to enable her to be with the group which most needs her attention at that particular time, also ensuring that the other children are helped as the need arises.

For smooth running she should make sure at the beginning of each day that all the children understand the apparatus and the work provided in each area and anything new must be explained thoroughly. A child who does not finish his work in any one area should not be stopped but should be able to remain in that area as long as necessary or if space does not permit, move to an unoccupied place in the classroom. This type of organization can be represented diagramatically as follows:

	Creative time	**Reading or word games**	**Maths or science**	**Writing**
AM				
1st half	Red group	Blue group	Green group	Yellow Group
2nd half	Yellow group	Red group	Blue group	green group
PM				
1st half	Green group	Yellow group	Red group	Blue group
2nd half	Blue group	Green group	Yellow group	Red group

If the social area for the day, or for the week, is organized round shopping, cooking and block play, the children who work there will be gaining much mathematical experience and need not work in the maths area unless there is a particular reason why they should do so. If the social area is organized around dramatic play, the children will be gaining language experience and need not work also in the writing area.

It is important to remember that the way in which a group's time is allocated should be varied from day to day; the red group should not always start the morning with creative activities nor write at the end of the afternoon and the other groups should vary their time accordingly. The teacher should also give some thought to the basis of groups within the class. Grouping according to ability must be avoided. It leads inevitably to streaming and this is not the object in an integrated day. A mixture of abilities and interests within a group creates a situation where the less able are encouraged to greater interest by seeing the work of brighter children and a better balance is struck within the group. At this point it can be emphasized that a child's *ability* to learn should not be confused with his *inclination* to learn — a child should not be left using his time unprofitably when with a little pressure he could be making greater progress.

If an integrated day organization is being introduced after working to a formal curriculum, it will probably be found that the easiest way is to start with only one group working more freely. More time can then be given to this group while the rest of the children are working more formally. This can lead gradually to the whole class working to a less formal pattern. Do not be disillusioned if the children do not record as much as may be expected by more formal methods. Some children within the group may be watching or discussing and this should not be discouraged but appreciated as being as valuable as recording. The children's observations, conversation and knowledge may sometimes surprise the teacher. If the teacher joins in with children's conversations and casually supplies the right words for what the children want to say, their use of words and vocabulary can be enlarged.

2 *Individual choice of activity*

Children choose their own work freely and there is no time limit. Before the children disperse to their various activities, they discuss as a group with the teacher the possibilities of any new material which has been provided that day and the work that is to be continued from the previous day. The children then decide for themselves in which order they will do their work and use the activities provided. Guidance, however, is necessary, especially with regard to the numbers of children able to work at one activity at a time.

In planning the work, one of the teacher's daily tasks is to ensure that there are enough activities and work places to occupy the children profitably. Teachers new to the integrated day have found it helpful to draw up each day a list of activities and the number of children who can be accommodated at each at any one time, and see that this number tallies with the number of children in the group. In order to provide for real choice, about ten extra activities and places should be provided so that there are always free spaces for children who have completed a piece of work. Such a plan, for a group of forty children, might look something like this:

Monday

Activity	**No. of chn.**	**Activity**	**No. of chn.**
Reading corner	4	Modelling with junk material	4
Word games	4	Music area	4
Writing table	6	Block building	2
Mathematics		Science area	2
structural material with work cards	4	Social area	
investigation of 3D figures	4	house	3
Group drama: puppet play (continued from Friday)	4	shop	2
Painting at easels (2)	4		17
Drawing with pencils and felt pens	3		
	33		

Total 33 + 17 = 50 choices

A common cause of difficulty in working an integrated day is failure to provide enough work and sufficient choice for the children, who become bored, idle or unruly instead of feeling stimulated and independent. After some experience, this kind of plan can usually be abandoned since the teacher will recognize how much her children need in order to be fully engrossed and will learn to interact with them in a more spontaneous way. But in the beginning, some such plan, varied from day to day, is undoubtedly helpful.

It is also helpful for the teacher to bear in mind that work in mathematics, art, reading, science etc. may also include writing and numeracy and that other activities encompass other skills. It is not by any means necessary for all writing to be done in the writing area or all mathematics in the mathematics room or corner. Every child need not visit every work area to gain adequate experience. For example, a child who chooses to paint may write an appropriate explanation of his picture or a story or poem about it. Most work cards involve reading. A child who makes models may use measurement to plan his finished object or may measure afterwards what he has made. He may be gaining new mathematical concepts of size, shape, volume and learning the appropriate words for expressing these. Recording work can be accepted as a piece of written work, or recording by speaking into a tape recorder or directly to the class is an acceptable piece of spoken English. Children should be free to move to different activities as soon as they have completed a task. The teacher must observe carefully that this conclusion has been reached in each case and a strict record must be kept of work done by each child (keeping records is dealt with in Chapter 9).

At the end of each session, or at least once daily, teachers usually call the children together to discuss their work. Of course, it is not necessary to review as a group everything that has been done, but children find great stimulus in hearing of special discoveries, viewing original paintings or models, listening to stories or poems written by other children. This is also a time for discussing problems, either those experienced by the whole class or by a particular group working on a project. Requests for information and special materials can also be made, so that the whole class can become aware of what is needed and can often help to supply it.

Many teachers claim that only method 2 is working in an integrated day from the children's point of view. Perhaps method 1 is a transitional mode of organization between formal teaching and full integration. As such, it may be helpful to teachers who are uncertain of their ability to sustain a fully integrated day, or who feel that their children cannot yet manage so much freedom. It may be regarded as a stepping stone to method 2 which allows the full integration of the teachers' and children's day.

Chapter 2

SCHOOL BUILDINGS

New buildings

Schools designed and built in recent years are often planned to encourage teachers of young children to organize their work within the less formal framework of an integrated day. The designs of the schools vary considerably but there are essential features arising from the demands of the integrated situation which all have in common. Fundamentally the term 'integrate' means 'to combine into a whole' which, when applied to school organization, demands *a degree of openness* in the building and a removal of physical barriers that have previously been regarded as traditional. Doors, stairs and passages, hitherto considered to be functional, are now found to be impediments to the free *movement* which is part of the integrated day. Children need to move freely as they change groups or work areas within their classroom; they need to move to other work spaces to consult different teachers; they need to be able to walk individually or in groups throughout the school to use the central library, the PE equipment or the resource-bay material.

The integrated day also requires that the building shall help to engender *cooperation* — between the teachers themselves; between children individually and in groups; between children and teachers. This factor has an effect on the siting and planning of staffrooms, classrooms and work areas. Whereas formerly the emphasis in school was on individual work, imposed discipline and silence, the integrated day places the emphasis on *socialization and communication* through speech, written language and visual arts. The building has to provide space where large and small groups can meet to discuss, to listen to music or stories, to watch television or to make and play tapes. This emphasis on communication also implies a need for places where children can withdraw into themselves for a time of quiet thought. Provision for communication through displays is also a required part of planning a building for the integrated day.

Modern infant or 'first' schools are seen as *workshops*, where active learning is pursued and where creative ideas can find expression. The concept of the school as a workshop implies that each child must have enough space for real work and access to functionally designed workrooms with adequate, accessible storage space.

Purpose-built schools

The whole concept of the integrated day can be reflected in the plan of a purpose-built school. The feeling of openness and the lack of barriers immediately give an impression of being able to work to an integrated pattern. Teachers have often complained that they felt shut in and cut off from their colleagues once the classroom door was closed. Today's architects, planning for integrated day schools, solve in various ways the basic problems of providing for the five main factors of openness, movement, cooperation, communication and work space. Included on pages 27 to 30 are the plans of four types of new schools, all specifically designed to facilitate the working of the integrated day. These designs indicate clearly that in the initial planning stages there has been close cooperation between the architects and those who will be working in the buildings.

All these schools are built on one level which encourages free movement for the children and better communication between the children and the staff. The hazards of stairways in infant schools have been removed and there is no longer the possibility of a class being isolated from the rest of the school in a classroom upstairs with the juniors. With junior schools often in the same building and on the same level there are improved facilities for communication between the teachers and children of both schools, or the school can fairly readily be switched from an infant/junior school to a primary school (five to eleven years) or a 'first' school (five to nine years). This is particularly advantageous since continuity of teaching and the passing on of records and information about children is greatly eased. As the children in the infant school or department are familiar with the junior school building, teachers and environment the transfer of children poses few problems. North Hill School (p. 27) will eventually become a full primary school for children aged five to eleven, working in one building under one head. The new block is planned to open out of the other end of the hall, and will contain a staffroom for all the teachers, and a studio for every class to use. In South Leas School

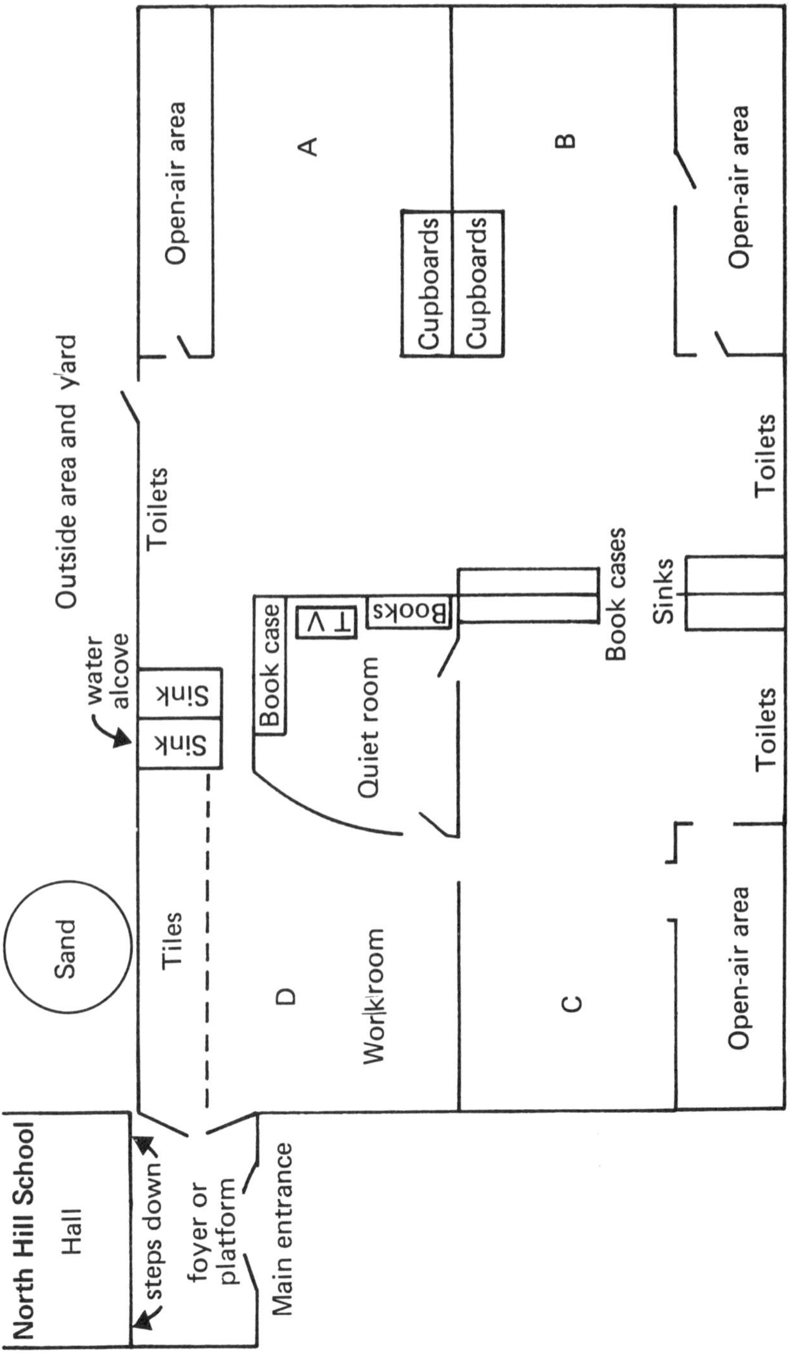

North Hill School
Hall
steps down
foyer or platform
Main entrance
Sand
Tiles
D
Workroom
C
Open-air area
water alcove
Sink
Sink
Book case
Quiet room
T V
Books
Book cases
Sinks
Toilets
Toilets
Outside area and yard
Toilets
Open-air area
A
Cupboards
Cupboards
B
Open-air area

South Leas School

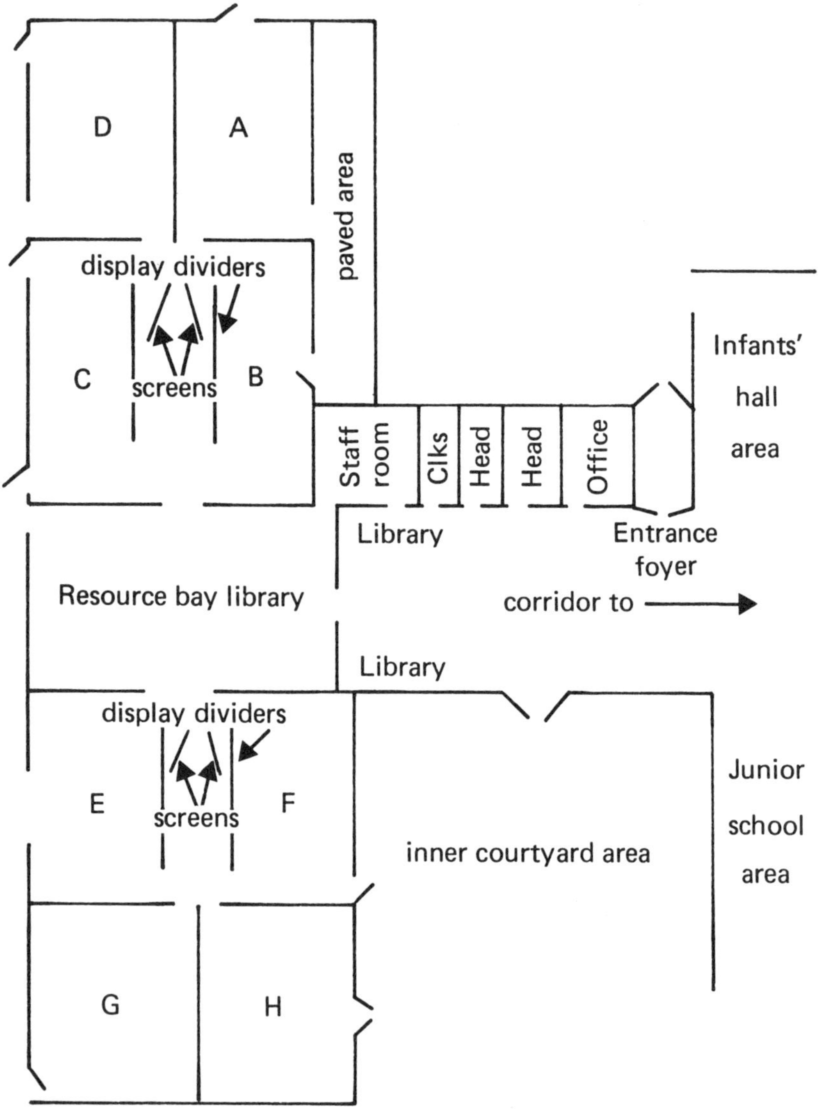

Classrooms A D G H closed; CBEF open plan

East Lake School

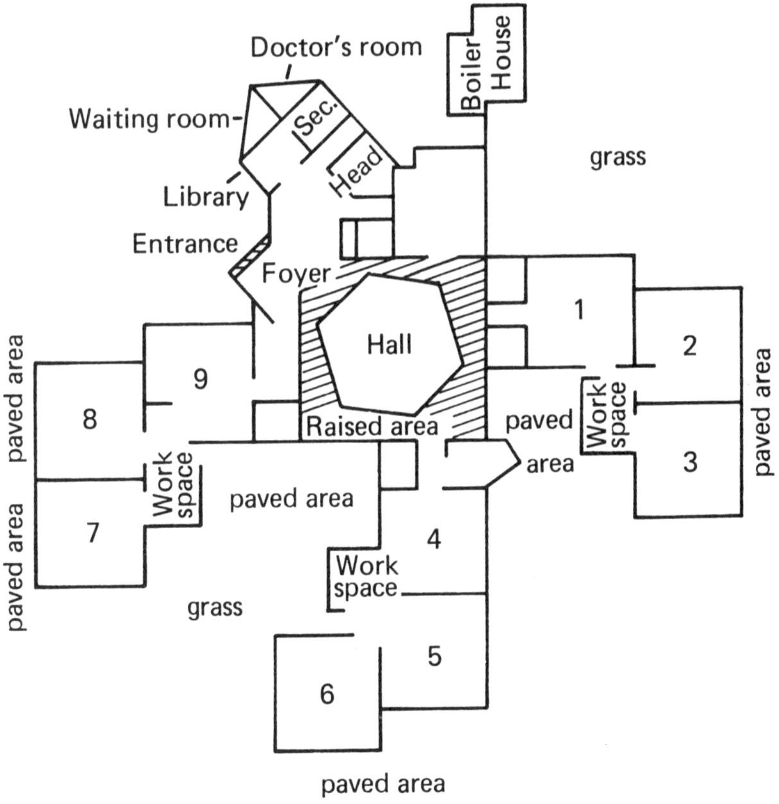

Classrooms 1,4 and 9 have direct access to hall.

B

West Vale School

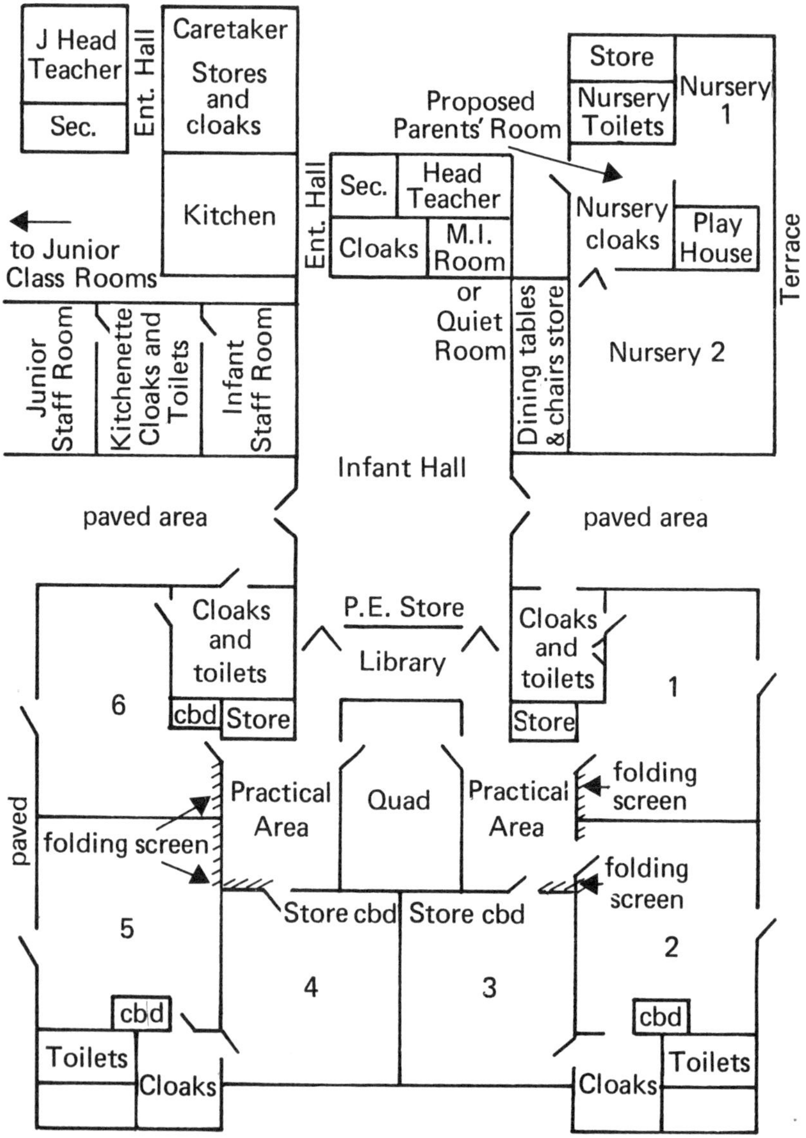

(p. 28) both infants and juniors use the same entrance, and although there are two separate headteachers, their offices are adjacent and they share secretarial assistants. The staffs of both schools share one large staffroom and kitchen. Cooperation between schools is made easy; non cooperation becomes very difficult.

Open-plan buildings are designed for movement between children and the various centres of the school. The problems presented by children having to pass through other classrooms are alleviated and corridors have been replaced by wider areas designed for practical work to be used in common by several classes. Classroom areas either have no doors and are simply designed as 'teachers' bases' or the division is made by double doors, sliding partitions or room dividers, so that the class area can be open or closed as required. At North Hill the school, designed for three classes, is almost completely open. There is provision for three teachers' bases (A, B and C) where the children meet their own teacher for registration, discussion and other group periods, but otherwise the whole teaching area is open to all, so that the children can move as their work requires to any section of the school. Each teacher can make use of the quiet room, either directly (room C) or indirectly (through D). Every room opens on to a covered verandah, the playground or garden. Each base has its own toilet facilities which can be entered from both inside and outside the building. There is one workroom (D) for all where practical activities, requiring special equipment can be carried out by individuals or groups, and this is open to the whole school though more easily accessible to children working with teachers A and C. At South Leas School, classes B, C, E and F occupy open-plan space, to which children in rooms A, D, G and H have access if their doors are left open. All children can use the library and resource bay quite freely since the room dividers in rooms C, B, E and F protect the teacher who is talking with her group from the movement of children down the central passage working space. The plan of East Lake (p. 29), designed for a nine-class school, does not solve the problem of free movement nearly as well. Children from rooms 1, 4 and 9 have free access to the facilities in the hall, library and foyer but the other classes have to pass through one of these three classrooms and, in the case of rooms 3, 5, 6 and 7, through the work space as well. In the plan of West Vale School (p. 30) it will be seen that complete freedom of movement is possible between the classrooms, the work areas, the library and the hall facilities. It is interesting to notice, however, that whereas in North Hill School and the eight-class South Leas the children and teachers can move freely throughout the whole school, and that where the doors are left open in rooms A, D, G and H no teacher or child is cut off from the others, in East Lake (nine classes) and West Vale (six classes), the school is broken into units of three classrooms. Referring back to Chapter I, it will be seen that these two schools therefore have the possibility of organizing the school in each of the four main ways, since this three-grouping of classrooms lends itself equally well to chronological grouping, transitional grouping, vertical grouping or team teaching. South Leas, with its possibility of two four-classroom blocks, was designed with the five to nine age range in mind and is therefore capable of the same variety of groupings. But North Hill lends itself above all to team teaching and would be a most difficult school to organize on chronological classification.

Emphasis on socialization and communication poses problems in the design of school buildings which have been met in various ways in the four different schools. In North Hill, particular attention has been given to the possibility of noise affecting the quality of work. Ceilings and walls are covered with sound-reducing tiles, and the floors are carpeted throughout. None of these custom-built schools was found to be noisy but the sound-proofing in this school is so effective that it is almost impossible to believe that 120 children are working and moving about the whole building quite freely. In this school, the problem of providing communication through books and visual arts has been met by lining the walls of the quiet room with pin-up boarding for displays and built-in shelving to house the school library. This room is also planned for the use of audio-visual aids and plugs for tape recorders, television and radio are provided.

At South Leas the provision for communication is absolutely central as the whole school revolves round the library and resource bays which are freely used by all. Here children from different classes meet as they work on individual or group projects and teachers exchange information or ask for help with problems throughout the day. Each classroom block is provided with two large areas for displays of work which are immediately visible and available for discussion by all four classes. At East Lake and West Vale, each block of classrooms has its own practical area where the adjoining groups of teachers and children meet and work together. In East Lake, the hexagonal hall is surrounded by a raised area where displays are set up, materials for scientific investigation are arranged and facilities are provided for group projects such as puppet-shows and dressing-up and devising plays. These facilities are available to children from all the classes who are thus able to meet informally, during individual or group work, children from other parts of this large school. In addition, there is a special library room for the children while the waiting room next to the doctor's room houses library and display material for the use of parents visiting the school.

The hall at West Vale is used in much the same way for music and science groups as well as for PE, but a feature of the planning of this school is the provision of television plugs and curtains in each classroom and the local authority has provided a number of portable sets so that each classroom can become where necessary a TV viewing room. The school library is the room specifically designed for quiet activities — books, pictures, using tape recorders, record players or just thinking — but in each of the four schools other areas have been adapted as quiet rooms. North Hill uses the area just inside the main entrance. This is a raised platform which serves as a stage when needed but can be furnished with moveable bookcases, chairs and tables for use as a reading and writing area. South Leas screens off small areas in the corners outside classrooms A, D, G and H. The foyer and the doctor's rooms in both South Leas and East Lake are used to make small, quiet reading rooms for children when not being used for their nominal function. These areas are much in use by children who appreciate a place to which they can withdraw by themselves.

A really comfortable room for teachers can promote a feeling of friendliness and relaxation which encourages the communication of ideas and the discussion of problems. Both South Leas and West Vale have large, comfortable, centrally-placed staffrooms with kitchens attached so that teachers are encouraged to remain in the building for all kinds of activities connected with their work.

The concept of the school as a workshop is greatly assisted in all four schools by the provision of practical work areas which help to remove messy work from the workshop area of the classroom and library. Classrooms in all four schools include carpeted areas and tables or wooden benches fixed to the walls where children may sit and read or write. These practical areas are all well equipped with sink units, power points and facilities for cooking. They have wooden benching at the children's own level and low cupboards for storing equipment. The provision in North Hill is particularly interesting as the whole work area is carpeted with the exception of a long tiled strip which is used by children who want to paint or make large messy models. In addition to the sink unit, there is also a tiled water-play alcove containing a small tiled paddling pool and two taps. South Leas has a practical biology area set up in the inner courtyard. This contains a large pond for the study of aquatic plants, birds and animals; there are built-in benches so that the children can sit quietly at any time to make observations. There are also trees and bushes specially planted to attract birds, butterflies and small animals which come in from the adjoining fields. This area has been designed for the school by the students of the local agricultural college.

A special feature of these purpose-built new schools is the attention which designers have paid to making the school hall attractive. Because of the loose structure of the integrated day in which children are mainly pursuing individual and group interests, the hall takes on an increased importance as a place where all meet together to share as a community in certain experiences. In the past, this focal point was too often cluttered with unsightly PE equipment and dining furniture. The three schools, North Hill, South Leas and West Vale, have built-in alcoves for PE apparatus and for dining tables and chairs, both alcoves hidden from the main hall by curtains.

The design of these schools with the integrated day in mind shows that architects have been led to understand the nature of the teachers' work and the children's modes of learning. It is obvious that a high degree of teacher-consultation has gone into preparing the plans for the new purpose-built schools.

Adapted buildings

Frequently old buildings are adapted to enable the teaching staff to use modern methods and to make a better use of the school for the development of the children. Conversions in old buildings are, however, only possible within a limited framework and the work is apt to be costly. Oldfield Infant School (see plan p. 35) gives some indication of the possibilities and limitations of adapting a really old school. Oldfield was first built in 1882 in response to the 1870 Education Act to serve a first-generation of universal education and a body of teachers which included both monitors and pupil-teachers. The whole ethos of the school was therefore different from anything that we can really conceive today. The status of teachers was lowly, the headteacher needed to exert constant

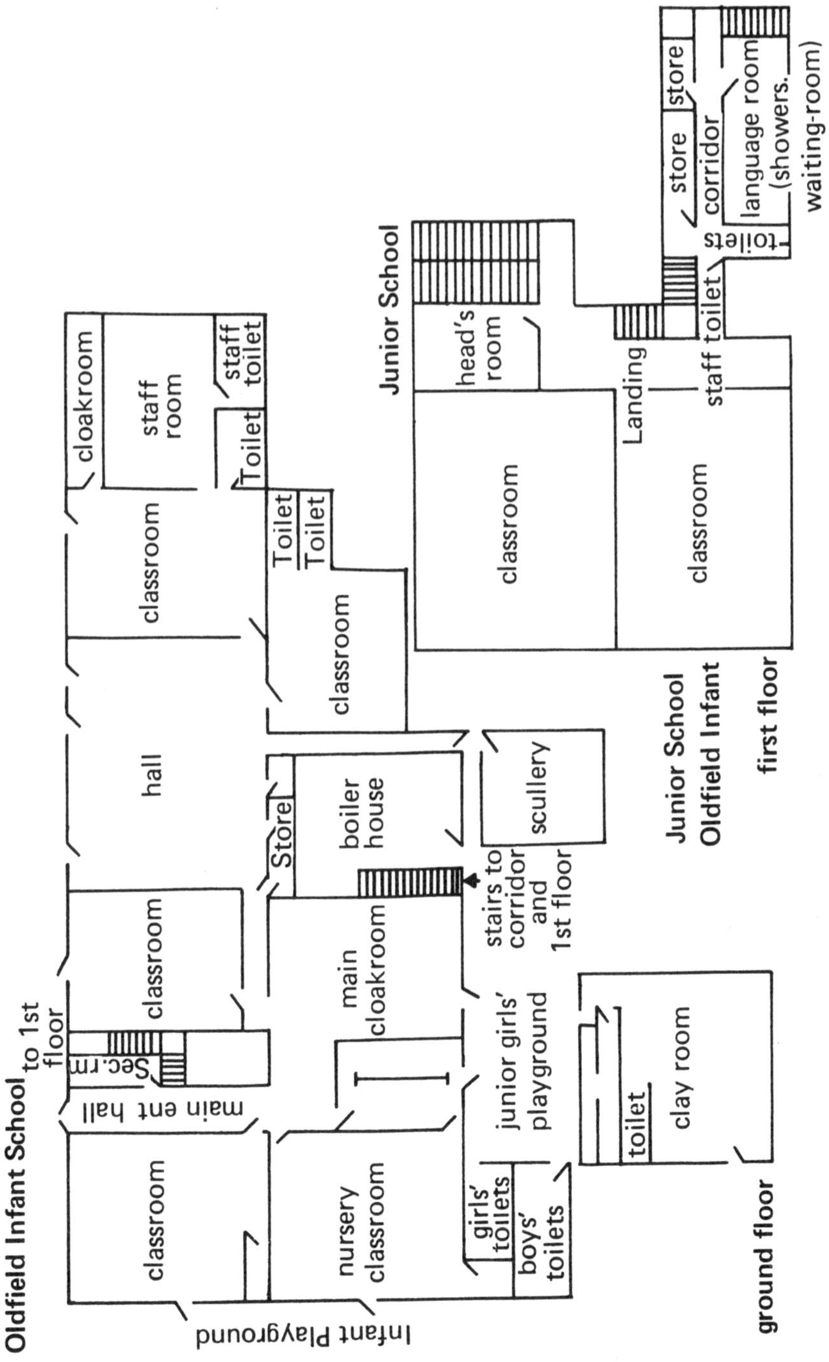
Oldfield Infant School
Infant Playground
classroom
main ent hall
Sec.rm
to 1st floor
classroom
hall
classroom
cloakroom
staff room
staff toilet
Toilet
Toilet
Toilet
classroom
Store
boiler house
main cloakroom
nursery classroom
girls' toilets
boys' toilets
junior girls' playground
stairs to corridor and 1st floor
scullery
clay room
toilet
ground floor
Junior School
head's room
classroom
classroom
Landing
staff toilet
toilets
store
store
corridor
language room (showers. waiting-room)
Junior School
Oldfield Infant
first floor

supervision and the school was designed to make this possible. Originally Oldfield consisted of two storeys. On the ground floor was the hall, with a gallery, and three classrooms, one on either side of the hall and the third where the staffroom, cloakroom and staff toilets are now. Almost immediately the entrance hall and two new classrooms were added. The first floor consisted of three classrooms. Between 1886 and 1963 various alterations were made to keep pace with educational developments. The gallery or galleries were removed and French windows were cut in walls of all the ground-floor classrooms. Four classrooms were enlarged, showers and a waiting-room were installed over the cloakroom and a roof playground was made. Since 1963 a considerable rebuilding programme has been undertaken. The shower waiting-room has been carpeted and adapted as a small room for teaching groups of immigrant children, with their own special toilets where the immigrants can learn western ideas of hygiene. In the main school, spaces have been found for indoor toilets and the outdoor toilets have been demolished. A passage, cut off from the main cloakroom, now connects the hall with the entrance hall. A secretary's room has been evolved from a store room and a classroom has been taken from the juniors and turned into a clayroom with a tiled floor, sink, french door and indoor toilet. Every classroom has been given a sink, formica tables, moveable cupboards and pinboard screens to form working areas, while a section of the room has been covered with thermoplastic tiles to provide a practical area. Each classroom has a carpeted area for reading and library activities.

Schools of the same age as Oldfield are often highly individual in design and what has been done here may or may not be applicable to other schools. But it can be seen that every effort has been made to adapt the building to modern requirements and the head and her staff run a highly successful integrated day in it. However, in some respects they are hampered by the building. Movement and communication between different rooms and children of different classes presents formidable problems, except in the case of the three classrooms centred round the hall and the two classrooms on the first floor, who can communicate only as they are grouped in the building or during assemblies in the hall. The library has to be housed in the very narrow entrance hall and on the first floor landing. Work spaces are confined to the classrooms except for the clayroom which all use but it also does double duty as a classroom. However, much has been done and within these limitations an excellent integrated day has been organized.

These old schools often have features which are helpful in organizing an integrated day and are appreciated by teachers. Rooms are usually large as they were originally built to house huge classes of sixty or more children, and there are frequently communicating doors or partitions between classrooms which makes team-teaching possible. (For example, Oldfield School originally had two interconnecting classrooms on the outer side of the hall, although one has now been converted to a staffroom.) There are often small rooms, nooks under staircases and odd corners which can be adapted for group work or quiet individual pursuits.

A later planning development was the 'central hall' type of school and examples of this can be seen in most English towns. This seems to be a most difficult type of building to adapt to modern methods of teaching. Originally some schools had classrooms which were only divided by moveable screens and these might have been useful in today's climate of team-teaching but, in general, we found that in line with the educational concepts of earlier decades, partitions had been replaced by solid walls without doors. However, some adaptation has been possible. In many schools, french windows now give direct access from the classrooms to a terrace or playspaces outside. Sinks have often been installed and sometimes there are tiled areas for activities involving water, clay and other messy materials. More display boards have been erected in many classrooms. Built-in storage space with open cupboards and drawers for paper and work books have been added to some schools. In one of the oldest buildings, which had a central hall and three floors, a start had been made in the nursery classes to adapt the space available to the requirements of an integrated day. Four rooms had been utilized for the nursery children who attended the school. In a previous conversion over twenty years ago, French windows had been added to each of these rooms to enable the children to go directly from their rooms onto the playground. In the more recent conversion, interconnecting doors between the four rooms had been removed and the doorways had been enlarged to allow the free passage of small children with big toys and trucks. Where differences of level had been encountered between the rooms, gently sloping ramps had been built to replace the original steps. Thus four rooms had become one big interconnecting unit for the very youngest children who need the maximum amount of play space. Additional and more adequate provision had been made for cloakrooms, toilets and showers. The new kitchen unit adjacent to the nursery classrooms was solely for the use of these four rooms, and separate from the main school kitchen. However, one of the main difficulties of this type of building is the lack of small spaces that can be turned into study areas.

Highthorpe School (p. 39) is an example of the verandah-type schools of the 1930s to 1950s. Structural changes that have been made in the post-war years adapt the school to more modern methods. The open verandahs have been glazed so that they can be used throughout the year for display and for communication between classes. Although they are not heated, for many months in the year they can be used also as work areas and during the winter for noisy or active occupations of short duration from which the children soon return to the warmth of the classroom. The old shower-room has been turned into a swimming pool, the pool itself having been provided by the Parent Teacher Association but maintenance undertaken by the LEA. When the school was built, a special room was provided as a workroom jointly for the staff and the caretaker but this has been converted into a science room for the children, and contains an oven and a sink. The staffroom now does double duty as a television room and blackout curtains and TV plugs have been installed. The entrance hall, which is heated, has been fitted up as a library with shelves, book trolleys, chairs and tables where children can read and write on individual projects. The music area is established at one end of the hall. Adaptations of Highthorpe building make the organization of the integrated day relatively simple except for the teacher in the outlying classroom between the swimming pool and the nursery, where communication with the main body of the school is difficult but this classroom was originally designed to be a second nursery in a nursery wing.

Actually the design of this school lends itself fairly well to team teaching and teacher cooperation with pairs of classes in the long corridor, but from this form of teaching the isolated classroom in the nursery wing would be necessarily excluded. Work space has been provided in each classroom with sink areas and carpeted reading areas but the glazed verandahs and the entrance hall give spaces for quiet individual work for at least half the year, depending on the weather. Highthorpe also has the possibility of being a fairly open school, for with some effort and proper training

Highthorpe School

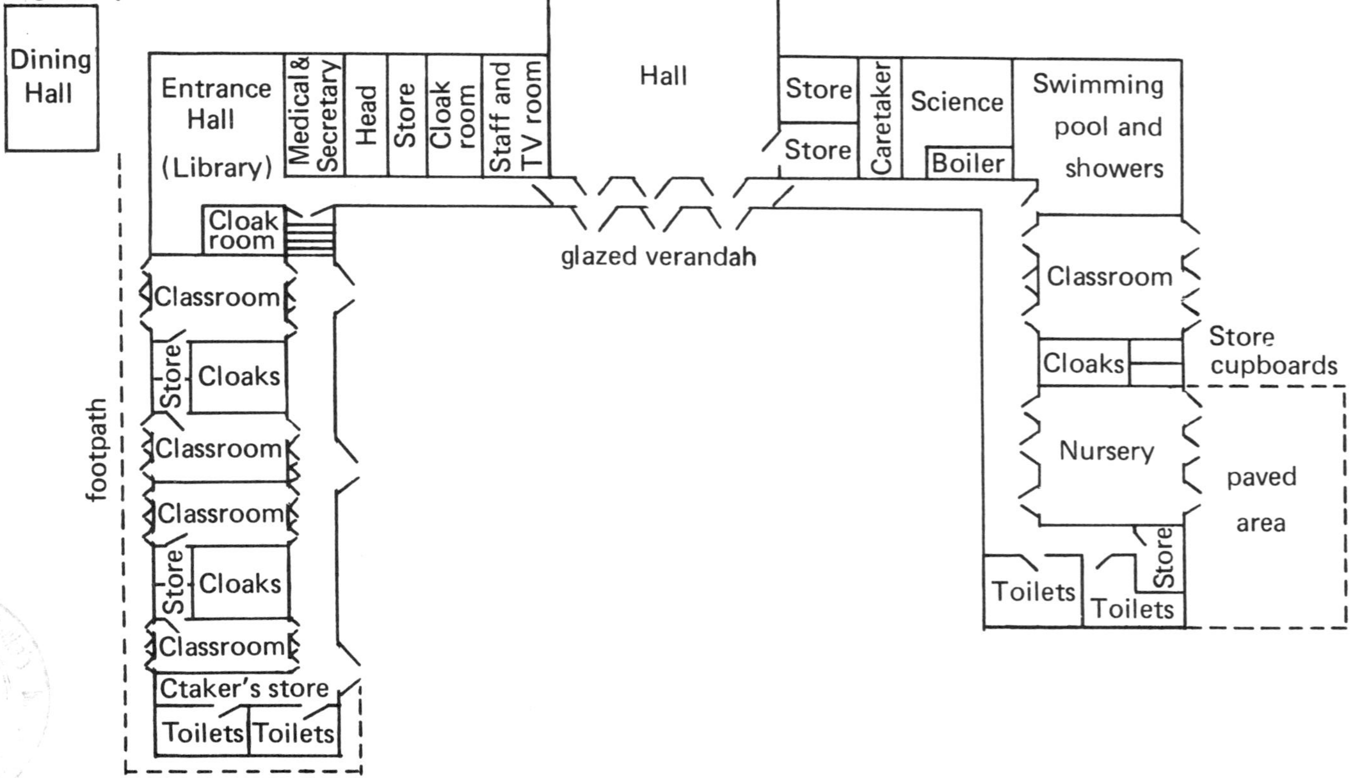

of children communication between all members of the school can be maintained; even the caretaker and the secretary are placed in the heart of the building, available to everyone and part of the whole community.

As money becomes available, school verandahs are being heated as well as glazed so that they can be used throughout the year. In some schools, each teacher uses her own piece of verandah as a classroom extension. In other schools, the space is used for communal activities in which children from all classes can join, e.g. the school café, bank, shops, library, art exhibition etc, while there are schools where the space is mainly used for displaying work done by different classes to act as a stimulus for the whole school.

The 'do-it-yourself' school

Many teachers who wish to work an integrated day pattern are teaching in old school buildings which have never been adapted to modern teaching methods. It is our experience that if the teacher is determined, it is possible to organize an integrated day under most teaching conditions. It is very difficult for staff themselves to make any significant changes in the school buildings and adaptations must largely be confined to the classroom (these will be dealt with in the next chapter). But certain changes are possible in the use of old fashioned school buildings where the staff is united, enterprising and willing to embark on a bit of do-it-yourself.

The idea of openness presents the first difficulty, since old schools were built to provide each teacher with a separate classroom which was her little kingdom. Twenty-five years ago it was considered an intrusion to enter another teacher's classroom and there were some classrooms into which no colleague ever penetrated. In many old schools, particularly the 'central hall' type, openness can sometimes be achieved by opening classroom doors. In some DIY schools, teachers have entirely removed the doors of certain classrooms, leaving others with doors to serve as quiet rooms. Within the rooms, doors have been removed from cupboards leaving open shelving to which the children have free access.

The foyer is the gateway between the outside world and school world. Teachers may consider how a feeling that the school is open to visitors may be shown in the school foyer and how the activities of the school may be displayed. Some schools arrange displays of school work in the foyer, with easy chairs and reading material about bringing up children. Other schools use the foyer as a working place for small groups of children, or as a room for storing, on open shelving, various kinds of interesting apparatus, books and work cards, so that visitors can see what is available to the children, who are often there choosing materials and able to talk about their activities. The school thus becomes open to visitors and is able to receive from them what they are able to give.

Freedom of movement is the next consideration. This may simply mean looking at the school furniture with a critical eye and altering its position, or more commonly storing material that will no longer be wanted. Sometimes superfluous furniture can be used to make more useful apparatus, e.g. old desks with the lids taken off and lined with polythene become aquaria; tall cupboards turned on one side with new shelves added become useful bookcases for the childrens' library. Movement paths around the school should be carefully observed and obstacles removed or repositioned. Where corridors are broken by steps, these can often be covered with ramps so that book trolleys, portable TV sets and wheeled toys can be moved without interruption.

To assist cooperation, common work and study areas may be devised and teachers often show great ingenuity in utilizing every small space. Cloakrooms can often be turned into spaces for television, or woodwork, or pottery since water is available. It is frequently possible to rearrange the cloakroom pegs so that more space is made available. In some schools, moveable coat racks have been brought back from the central education store, and the children's clothing is dispersed to different parts of the school after assembly, leaving the cloakrooms free to be used as work rooms. Where the traditional playtime has disappeared with the coming of freedom to the classroom this use of the cloakroom is not too difficult. In schools with closed verandahs or long corridors, it is possible to pull the moveable coat racks across the verandahs as dividers to create work areas. In any case, where the school has verandahs and corridors, these need no longer be wasted as transit space but used for displays, and where they are wide enough as areas for noisy or messy work. Where corridors are narrow, they may be adapted to reading and writing activities by hinging table tops and wooden seats to the wall. Again, staircases in very old schools can be covered with pinboarding for picture exhibitions, and book troughs fixed to the walls can hold attractive reading matter. In one school we found children sitting on mats down one side of the stairway, quietly reading. Small rooms can often be adapted to surprising uses. A caretaker's brush cupboard has become a science room where small groups can work together.

Medical rooms make libraries and writing rooms apart from the doctor's infrequent visits, while shower rooms with their water taps become excellent areas for practical activities.

Many heads now take over part of large, old-fashioned halls as a communal study area for groups of children from various classes. Here the head organizes some field of study in which she is interested or in which the school would be otherwise deficient, and invites children to work with her there. These areas may be shut off from the main body of the hall by screens, clothes horses covered with material or dividers made from discarded furniture. Effective dividers can be made from very large cardboard boxes (of the kind used in supermarkets for customers to pack their purchases in). These box-dividers give surprisingly good wear and also act as extra cupboards.

The plan (p. 43) of Middleway School shows a central-hall type of building and how one headteacher and her staff have adapted it to the needs of the integrated day. Middleway is a peculiarly difficult building because there are only two possible exits in case of fire, one through the main entrance and another through the French windows in the nursery. Owing to the rise of the ground, it has not been possible to cut French windows in the outside walls of the classrooms. This means that the main entrance must be left completely uncluttered and it is impossible to set up the usual library facilities here. The toilets open out of the cloakroom which is therefore rendered unsuitable for painting and clay work. The classes cannot easily communicate since this would involve children walking through PE lessons, which is dangerous, for the position of ropes and other agility material is fixed by suspension from the roof and cannot be altered. And yet as the plan shows, much has been done by the head and staff of Middleway to make it possible for each teacher to organize a successful integrated day giving children from each class the chance to work with children from other classes in the hall resource areas or the science, art and mathematics bases.

If the staff are willing to undertake the extra work implied in running an integrated day, they may want to make their staffroom as comfortable as possible so that staff meetings and discussions can be carried on in a relaxed, sociable atmosphere. If the LEA has been unable to provide many comforts, the teachers can do it themselves. It is wonderful how many husbands will help and how easily old but comfortable chairs, carpets and curtains can be obtained by asking around.

Middleway School

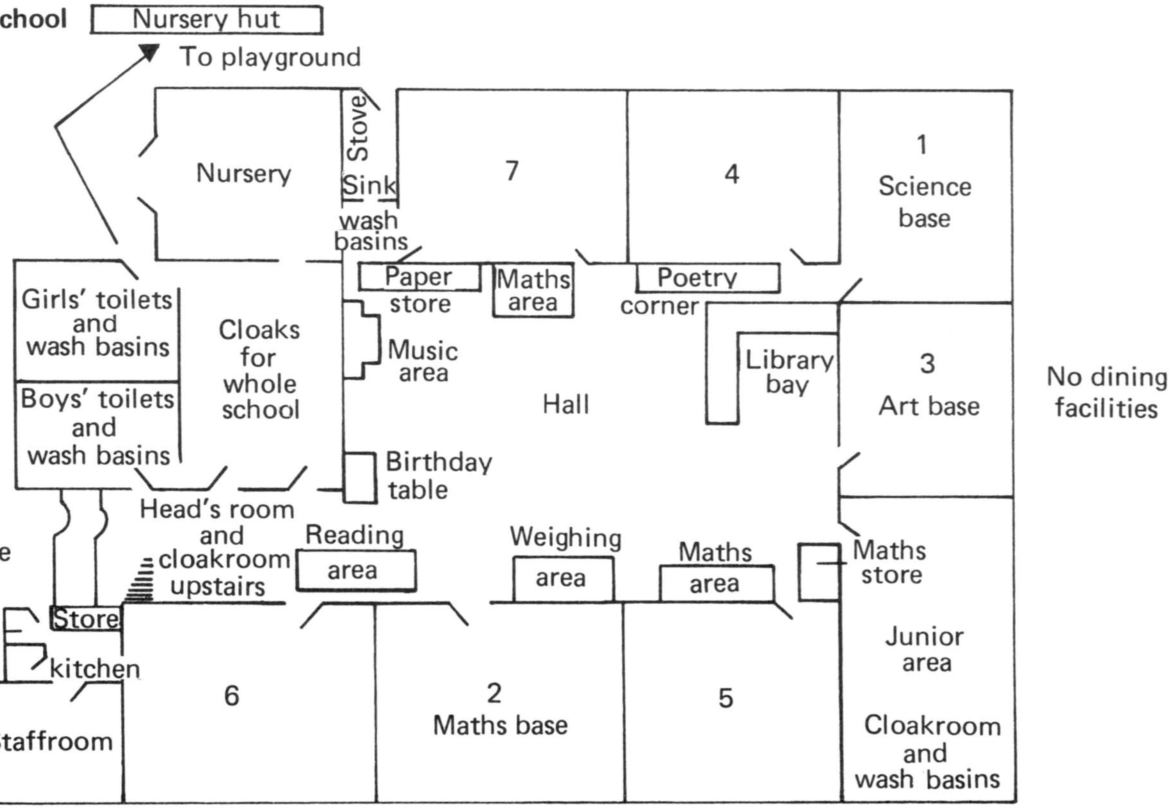

Chapter 3

THE ORGANIZATION OF WORK AREAS

Teachers with whom we discussed the problems of starting an integrated day agreed that the first step was to take a long, hard look at the classroom, to decide what they wanted to have in it and where everything could be put. In rooms crowded with tables and chairs there was not enough space so teachers removed as much furniture as possible to create free areas. A seat and table space for each child were seldom considered necessary, but in every school each child had somewhere readily available to keep his personal possessions. In the newer schools, special furniture to hold each child's books, shoes, lunches and small belongings was either built-in or provided as part of the initial equipment. In established schools teachers had invented many ingenious ideas to provide these individual 'putting places'. Some of these ideas were:

1 Seed trays, painted or stained and labelled with each child's name. These are easily stackable.
2 Canvas wall pockets, labelled with children's names. These were hung from hooks on peg boarding or from picture-display battens of suitable height.
3 Wooden shoe-lockers no longer used in cloakrooms were screwed together to make firm pigeon-holes.
4 Plastic vegetable racks, with individual pull-out trays.
5 Oblong plastic washing-up bowls or butchers' meat boxes, which are easily stacked and kept clean.
6 Dexion or Tabrax shelving.
7 Strong cardboard packing boxes of uniform size which have been built up into a pigeon-hole unit, glued together and painted.

Much thought had been given to the extension of the classroom, as the integrated day needs a great deal of space, and as many areas for work and activities as can possibly be contrived.

Classrooms had been extended by making full use of corridors, verandahs, cloakrooms, halls (see Chapter 2), but in each case careful consideration had been given as to how this extended space could be used. In some schools, quiet activities were retained in the classroom while noisier, messier activities had been distributed into the extended classroom, while in other schools the reverse policy had been adopted, but in general each school did its best to separate the quiet and studious from the noisy and messy.

When teachers had decided how the maximum amount of effective space could be created, they commonly found that the next consideration was the number and kinds of work areas that were needed. Integrated day classrooms need work bays, working surfaces and storage spaces. In the most modern schools these practical areas have been provided as part of the building, but in older schools teachers have had to use their ingenuity. Teachers had used the following devices to create spaces for activities:

1 Cupboards and low lockers were moved across the room at right angles to form work bays.
2 Nursery towel racks were covered with pegboard or canvas to form both display and storage units and also to act as room dividers.
3 Three-sided folding book cases or other types of book units were commonly used as dividers for reading areas.
4 Clothes horses covered with hessian, canvas or pegboard can serve as display or storage units. A clothes horse tied between

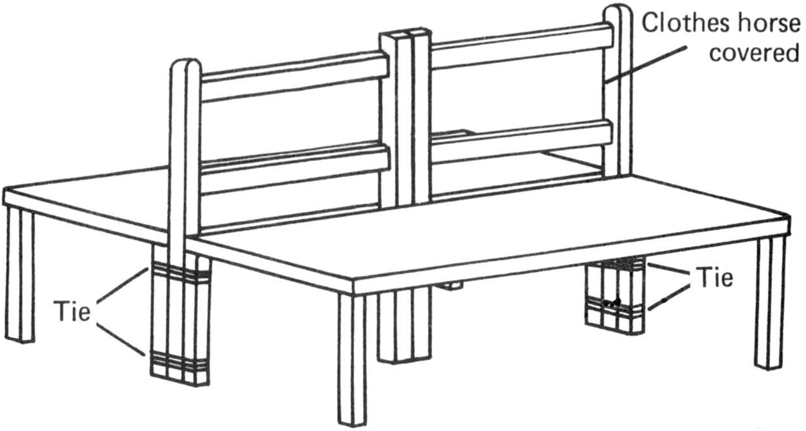

two tables made a room divider, a display area and two study booths at the same time.

5 Tall cupboards with doors taken off and fitted inside as shelves made both storage spaces and room dividers.

6 The teacher's table with the legs cut down made both a strong work table for clay or other construction work and divided off a work area. In other schools, the teacher's table had been fitted with hardboard or curtains all round to make both a display area and a Wendy House where little children could pursue the favourite game of house-under-the-table, as they do at home. In one school this had become a pirate cave and in another an underwater home. The teachers in these schools either used the table top only or were provided with a small wall bureau for their own work.

7 Moveable blackboards, either covered or painted or else left black, for children to draw on.

8 Rolls of corrugated card which can be unrolled to the required length; pictures can be attached by ordinary sewing pins.

9 Screens made from Tri-wall three-ply cardboard.

Free access to work areas posed the problem of storing material and equipment so that it could be easily fetched and put away by children as required. In the new schools this did not present great difficulties where there was a balanced amount of both fixed and moveable furniture, most of which was at the children's own level, and the work benches which lined the walls had ample storage space underneath. Clay could be stored under the bench used for that activity, fixed book units held displays of books and mobile book trolleys had compartments for storing the greater proportion of the class books. There were moveable blackboards and specially designed room dividers, and several schools had huge painting boards with special surfaces which were shared by several classes. Stock cupboards either opened off each classroom or were centrally placed in the schools where the heads had made them generally available to the staff. But in older schools teachers had displayed much inventiveness in grappling with the storage problem:

1 Doors to cupboards had been removed and the shelves lined with American cloth, Fablon, or painted.

2 Vegetable racks were used as storage units for collage materials, mathematics equipment, etc.

3 Plastic laundry baskets stored bricks. A wheeled brick-truck was made from the bottom of a discarded pram on which a strong canvas bag was hung.

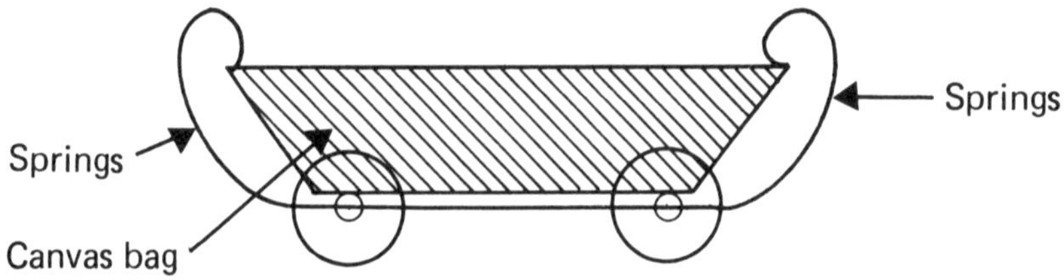

4 Cardboard or plastic boxes fitted into a sand tray provided storage for sorting and collage materials.

5 Collapsible 'high and dry' clothes horses were used for drying paintings while other teachers put up clothes lines across the room and pegged the paintings out, which looked very attractive and gay.

6 Sets of wall pockets held such items as writing paper, work cards, small books and word lists. Cheap plastic wall pockets designed for holding shoes were found particularly useful for reading material of all kinds since the transparent plastic does not hide the nature of the contents. They can also be used for the smaller dressing up properties.

7 Moveable nursery cloakroom stands or towel racks proved useful for storing dressing-up clothes while the shoes accompanying the costumes were hung underneath. In some large classrooms it had been possible to bring in an old wardrobe to store costumes, while a few teachers had been successful in obtaining interesting storage equipment from dress shops that were closing down. Clothes airers and stocking driers have also been found useful for hanging dramatic costumes, while accessories such as flowers, feathers, beads and laces have been stored in plastic bags where they are protected but visible.

8 Plastic bins housed clay and were found to be very convenient but large, strong, plastic bags, such as those used for garden peat, have been found useful if the top is turned over and fixed with bulldog clips to exclude air. Plastic bins have also been used for junk material, bricks, collage fabrics, bulk food for pets, etc.

9 Plastic trays were sometimes used instead of work surfaces, particularly for modelling activities and for preserving large

jig-saw puzzles throughout the time that the children were working on them.

The classroom diagrams on pages 49 and 50 show how two teachers adapted their rooms to the necessities of the integrated day. One room was part of a verandah-type school and the other a mobile classroom addition to an old school building. The first teacher adopted the plan of putting messy activities as far as possible out on the verandah whereas the second teacher puts children who need quiet for writing outside in the cloakroom — not ideal but the only classroom extension available to her.

Teachers often find that it is not necessary to have every single infant school activity available in their own room. Some activities can be shared with another cooperative teacher, some are frequently placed in other parts of the school (see Chapter 4) and children sometimes show a fluctuating interest in others so that when interest is waning, teachers can decide to replace some activities with other occupations. However, there are some areas of work for which school policy will decide that provision must always be made and some of the more constant activities are listed in this chapter with suggestions made by experienced integrated-day teachers. These teachers also generally made the point that they found it essential to avoid making a fixed room plan, and preferred to have a daily or weekly room plan in mind as the work or children's interests vary, and then to make time before the start of each day's teaching to prepare the room and materials. Some teachers may be tempted in the beginning to put out too much which may create a muddled situation for both teacher and children although the provision of a nucleus of basic, constant activities helps to stabilize the children's classroom world.

Reading and writing areas

In the schools visited, every effort had been made to provide reading and writing areas that would be both comfortable and functional so that the children were attracted to the occupations provided. Some classes had been provided with carpets for this area and North Hill School was carpeted throughout so that children could, if they wished, sit on the floor to read. In less fortunate schools teachers had often made their own provision by bringing along old carpets, or buying carpet squares which are sold quite cheaply as old pattern samples in most carpet shops. Little stools or chairs from educational manufacturers had often

Plan of a classroom arrangement 1 (older children)

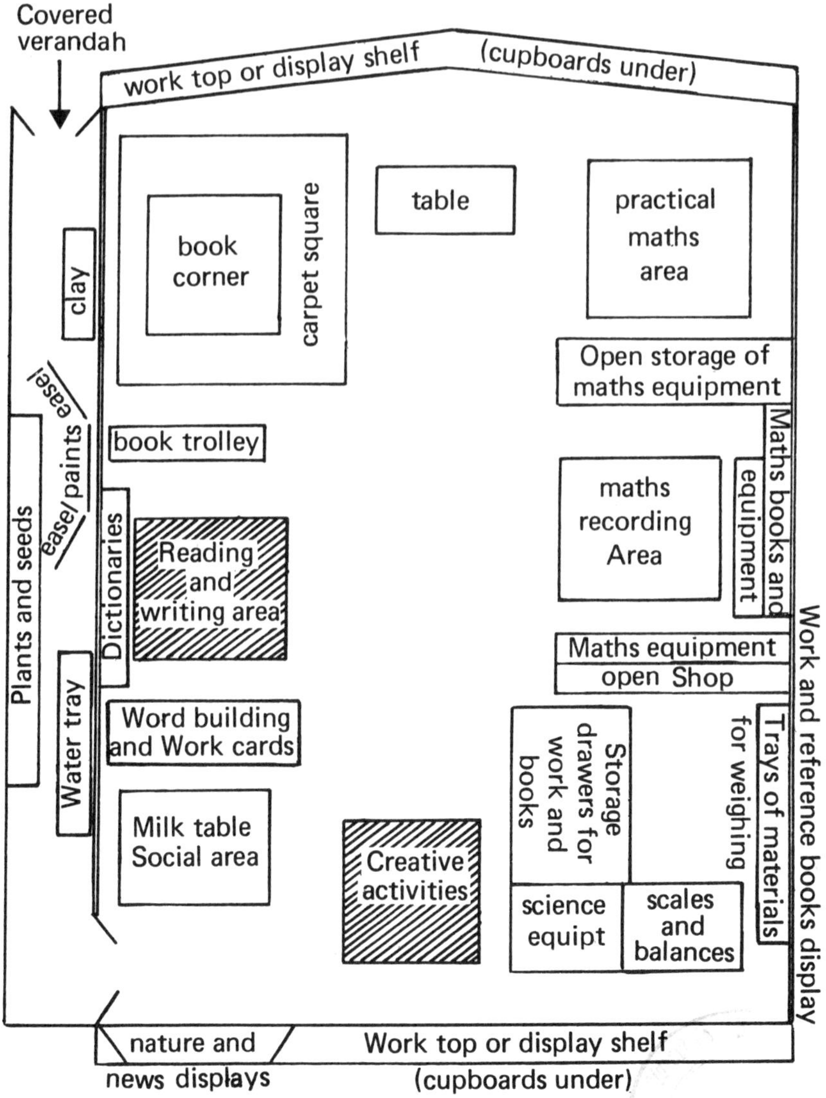

Plan of a classroom arrangement 2 (younger children)

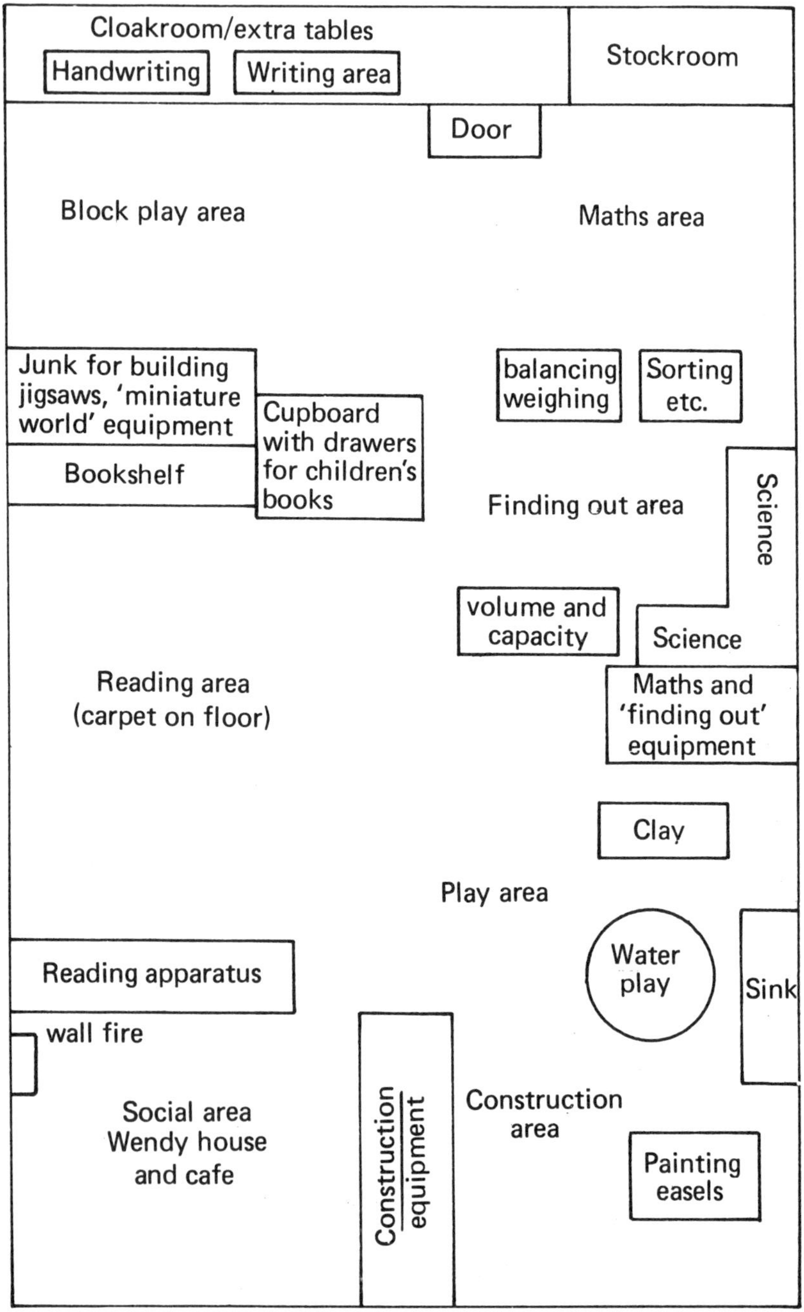

been supplied but other interesting forms of seating were noted:

1 Wooden boxes painted by the children and covered with hessian over foam rubber made comfortable stools.
2 Discarded motor-scooter tyres with cushions to put in the centre provided informal seating; the cushions were sometimes stitched by children and stuffed with foam rubber pieces.
3 Some teachers had special opportunities for obtaining old seats from buses, caravans, cars etc.
4 Chairs had been made from wooden boxes or tubs, which were sawn at about the half-way mark as shown. The seats were covered with foam cushion. The children then covered the seats with papier mâché and painted them.

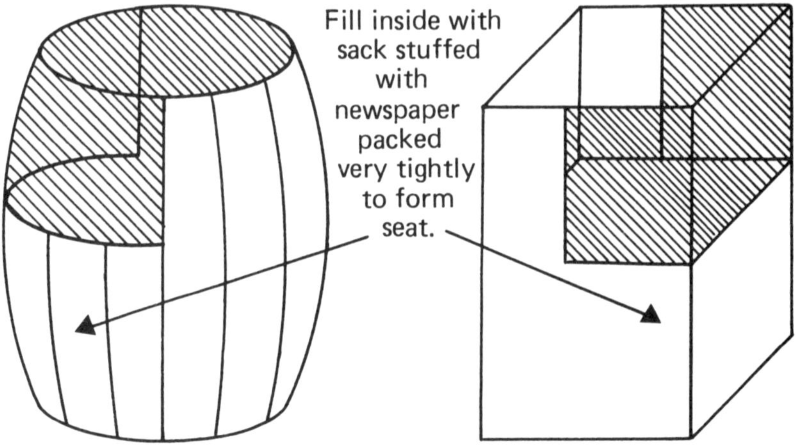

These chairs are very strong and long lasting. The bottom half in one school was covered with a 'petticoat' of material gathered onto elastic and these chairs looked particularly attractive.

5 Some teachers had been able to obtain old armchairs or settees by appealing to parents and friends. Sometimes a child's small armchair or hassock was given to the class when a child had outgrown it at home.

In setting up the reading and writing area, teachers had devoted much thought to displaying and storing the various kinds of books and materials that are required so that they were visible and readily accessible. The various kinds of books that teachers had to provide for seemed to be:

1 books on display to stimulate interest
2 books of reference, information books and dictionaries
3 books belonging to the school reading schemes
4 books for free reading for pleasure
5 books made by the teacher and children.

In addition, a variety of reading and writing apparatus was usually provided:

1 reading apparatus
2 reading games
3 word cards, comprehension cards, work cards
4 writing cards
5 paper and books for writing.

Before deciding how to store this equipment teachers generally worked out a policy for using the material. Library areas or book corners were usually placed in a quiet part of the classroom. Some teachers separated the quiet reading area from the word study and writing area which is rather more active and noisy, as young children frequently like to talk about their writing. In the diagram on p. 49 it will be seen that this is the policy adopted by the teacher, and that the two areas are separated by the book trolley which contains books for pleasure reading on the book-corner side and books of information on the side facing the reading and writing area. The diagram on p. 50 shows the teacher taking the writing activities with appropriate work cards and dictionaries right away from the reading area and establishing it in the cloakroom outside the classroom. Another school in an educationally deprived area provided a permanent table for Word Bingo just inside the classroom door where groups of children practised word-recognition on a rota system throughout the day, and this was quite separate from both the reading area and the writing area which were in other parts of the room. We found that the problem of placing the reading and writing area was common to all schools but that each teacher had solved it in her own way. The quiet corner of the room was not always devoted solely to reading and writing but a place might be found for a box of slides and a viewer or for a tape recorder which could be used turned down low or with headphones for telling a story or reading a book which children followed in their own copies. Schools which owned a Language Master often placed it among the word-study materials.

Teachers aimed to display picture books in ways that were

attractive to children. In many schools the tops of cupboards, shelves or window ledges were used, but where space was limited books were shown on stands fitted into pegboard or racks and book cases fastened to the walls. In the newer schools wall-mounted book stands were fitted to save classroom space for other activities. Where display space was very limited indeed, a few interesting books were selected for show while the others were stored in book boxes. Sometimes these were classified and books were related to their appropriate boxes by coloured labels. Display stands chosen from the various educational catalogues were used in many cases to hold open books, and pages were held down with rubber bands. Blue-Tack — a colourless Plasticine-type of material — was used to display pictures as this would not damage the corners of wall pictures from reading schemes nor the painted walls.

Books designed for individual reading were usually arranged attractively in book units chosen from the great variety shown in manufacturers' catalogues. In one small school where money was very scarce, a book unit had been made from a three-sided clothes horse backed with pegboard. Narrow shelves had been nailed onto the horizontal bars and expanding curtain wires stopped the books from falling. Inside this little 'room' were placed a rug, two stools and a small table. The pegboard outside was used for displays. We also saw a moveable book unit made from an old blackboard on castors with shelves fixed on both sides to brackets which were screwed into the wooden frames.

The books belonging to the school reading schemes seemed, on the whole, to be kept in some central store, sometimes in bookshelves in the head's room, sometimes in cupboards in the staff room, and sometimes in the general school stock room. In some schools teachers themselves drew out what they needed for their children, in other schools each child returned the reading book individually to the head, read a few words or sentences and was given the next book on the school reading scheme. Other schools stored the books they used in shoe boxes or strong cardboard boxes in the classrooms. If placed on lockers or work bench tops they were easily accessible.

The storing and display of books written by teachers and children, i.e. 'made books', always presents difficulties since they are usually large and floppy. We saw many solutions to this problem of which the most satisfactory seemed to be:

1 hanging from suction hooks fixed to woodwork

2 hanging from golf tees stuck into peg boarding
3 displayed on magazine racks
4 fastening with bulldog clips to a tape stretched from top to bottom of the side of a French window
5 displaying the latest book open on a small table like a lectern, with the other 'made books' piled underneath on a tray so that children could bring out any book needed for reference.

Reading apparatus, work cards and writing cards were often stored in wall pockets of various kinds though some teachers used stacked and labelled boxes. A few teachers provided writing boards with clips for securing the paper so that children could write about the things that interested them in any part of the room. If the children did not keep their writing books and papers individually in their own lockers, there was usually a box in the writing corner to store all the books, together with some form of indexing (e.g. by colour) so that each child could find his own book quickly. The writing area always contained one or two tables or a table top hinged to the wall, the amount of writing space depending on how each teacher planned the writing activities of the class. Sometimes the library area contained a table on which the children could rest large books but sometimes it did not as carpets or mats allowed children to look at these books on the floor.

All the teachers that we saw had some way of training the children to think of this reading and writing area as a quiet place where talking was permitted but voices must be kept low and chattering was discouraged. Some had signs prominently displayed as in a public library — 'Quiet please' — others limited the number of children in the area by written notices, 'Six children can read here', while other teachers simply aimed to build up a particular attitude towards library areas in the children for whom they were responsible.

Mathematics area

It is often helpful to site the mathematics area next to the science and nature area, as materials provided for counting, measuring and recording in mathematics are frequently also needed in children's scientific activities, while scientific observations and experiments can provide a basis for much work in mathematics. In both the classroom plans included in this chapter, mathematics and science areas have been juxtaposed with mutual benefit.

In planning the mathematics area, teachers had commonly

considered very carefully the ages of the children for whom they were planning and the kinds of work that would be likely to be achieved. Classroom 2 (p. 50), designed for younger children, provides two practical mathematics areas. The first contains material for building basic number concepts of grouping, counting, sorting and measurement, the second is a finding-out area where these concepts and materials can be used in mathematical and scientific investigation and discovery. Many of the older children for whom classroom 1 (p. 49) is designed will have progressed to the stage of recording their discoveries and a special area is provided containing chairs and tables at which children can write, make graphs, diagrams or pictorial records, together with storage drawers for holding work books and paper of various kinds. Older children are often ready to follow a planned progression in their mathematical work and shelves are also provided to hold mathematics textbooks and boxes of work cards.

With children in first schools mathematics is generally thought of as falling into two main streams of investigation, each of which requires its own kind of equipment. First, the study of the structure of our number system, for which various kinds of structural material are provided. There are many sets of such material on the market and each school usually decides on two or three schemes of structural apparatus, since teachers find that more than one type is desirable as each set has its own particular strengths and weaknesses which need supplementing. For example, Cuisenaire provides a mass of material for studying the composition of numbers whereas Stern with fewer number blocks has the 1 to 100 number track which is not available in Cuisenaire. Many of these schemes of structural mathematics have accompanying work books for children and teachers. We found that frequently teachers had taken these books to pieces, mounted the pages on cardboard and covered them with Shireseal or paper-varnish to make work cards.

Structural material is often very expensive and instead of buying complete sets for each class, many schools keep it in a central store or reservation area, from which teachers can draw what is immediately needed by their children. Other variations were that in one school the material was kept on open shelves in the main corridor where teachers could see it as they passed up and down. In Middleway School (Chapter 2) a room was equipped as a mathematics room which was shared by all classes. East Lake School had a scheme by which the assembly hall was given up on Wednesdays to the large mathematical material such as number tracks, and children from every class were allocated time to use it throughout the day. Many schools add to their initial structural equipment by making their own, and most school suppliers' catalogues contain suggestions for materials that can be used in this way. Teachers also seem to make considerable use of pegboard with various kinds of pegs for making many kinds of counting, grouping and geometrical apparatus. We found much use of ridged hardboard which manufacturers have conveniently made in 25 mm wide ribs and is therefore very useful for making rulers and cutting strips or squares which can be the basis of so many structural schemes.

The second stream of mathematical discovery might be called 'environmental mathematics' as it helps children to gain an understanding of the use of number and measurement in everyday life. We found that teachers provided much of the necessary material themselves — cardboard boxes, cotton reels, clothes pegs, old telephone books, timetables, AA books, stamps, discarded handbags for shopping etc, though some materials such as telephones, coins for shopping, balances, measures of all kinds were usually provided by the school from the wealth of materials illustrated in suppliers' catalogues. Most teachers said that they had formed a habit of never throwing anything away but devoted much thought to how things could be used in the childrens' investigations. In dealing with environmental mathematics, there seemed to be two approaches; first, from the mathematical experience in the environment that the children are trying to master, e.g. weighing, measuring, paying for things, and second from a problem in the environment which can be solved mathematically, e.g. is it quicker — or further — to go this way or that? How many chairs can we fit in for the audience for our play? To approach the subject in the first way teachers usually provided real-life material such as different kinds of measures, balances, timepieces, coins, goods to be sold, while the second approach commonly needed tools such as stop-watches, trundle wheels, surveyors tapes etc.

This wealth of material calls for careful organization and storage and we found that the most successful mathematics areas seemed to be those where all the apparatus was both easily accessible to the children and clearly labelled, so that any child could be quickly directed towards the specific material necessary for solving his particular problem. We found most teachers provided as a minimum:

1. Many types of containers, and the variety of washable polythene boxes, trays, bowls, bottles, cutlery trays, baskets and bins seemed very useful in teaching mathematical concepts of size and shape as well as providing storage.
2. A nearby store of plain and coloured papers, squared paper, 100-squared sheets of paper, gummed coloured paper, graph paper, lined paper, checked paper etc.
3. Small items of equipment such as pencils, rulers, paper, rubbers, scissors, crayons, as well as mathematical tools such as compasses, set-squares, adding machines, and other tools mentioned in the previous paragraph.
4. Boxes ready-filled with collections for sorting into sets by colour, shape, material, texture, use etc, stored together with hoops or rope rings into which they can be sorted and grouped.
5. Collections of flat shapes and boxes of every possible shape which can be used for building, filling with sand or beans, sorting or grouping, to help children form geometrical concepts and concepts of volume.

The floor may often be the best work space provided that it is in the mathematics bay and out of the main traffic routes, though even with young children most teachers find a need for one place for writing where some recording can be done or delicate work be achieved safely.

Social area

As this is the area where children are expected to talk and discuss, it is noisier than any of the other work areas however controlled the voices that are used. This presents problems in placing the area within the classroom and some schools such as East Lake and West Vale (Chapter 2) place this area outside in the corridor or in the communal work space. Two schools had converted the medical room into permanent children's houses that could be used by any groups as required. In the plan of the mobile classroom (p. 50) for younger children it can be seen that the teacher has placed such value on social opportunities for very young children that she has provided three different social areas — one for block play, one near the sink for water play and a third area for home activities in a warm corner near the wall fire. In the classroom for older children (p. 49) the social area is near the door and although it is perhaps rather too close to the reading and writing area for comfort, it is well away from the book corner and the mathematics recording area, and has the advantage of easy access for the caretaker with milk crates and easy exit for these older children wanting the wider experience of socializing with children in other classes.

Naturally, the equipment which can be provided in the social area is limited by the space available but teachers often use the same floor space for a succession of different themes. Nearly all schools provide a home area with provision for playing-out the home activities of both men and women and simulating the real home as nearly as possible. Equipment that is commonly available includes:

1 Dressing-up clothes and accessories such as hats, handbags, purses, aprons, sewing and knitting materials for girls, and caps, hats, handyman's apron, a pipe, carpentry tools for boys. Where a mirror is provided, there seems to be a greater interest in dressing up and dramatic play.
2 Suitably dressed dolls, including an Action Man for the boys, with a doll's pram, cot and bath, bedlinen and towels.
3 A table, chairs, tablecloths, tea set and a box of cutlery; some schools are also able to provide an easy chair.
4 Food, which can be either simulated or real things to eat cooked by the children.

Simulated food

1 Pictures cut from magazines and mounted on stiff cardboard or picnic plates.

2 Food modelled from a mixture made from one part salt to three parts flour by volume, mixed with water to a stiff dough, dried in a slow oven or over a radiator and painted. (This mixture makes a very strong and permanent modelling material.)

3 Swiss roll and sandwich cakes made from foam rubber.

Real food

Some schools have a cooker which the children can use to do their own cooking, however simple, and these schools are usually able to encourage children to bring some of their own cookery ingredients, which are then put into containers and labelled. The children build up over a period their own cookery books.

5 Cleaning materials such as a brush and dust-pan, polish, dusters and mops. In some schools we found carpet sweepers.

6 Telephone and telephone books, either old GPO books or class telephone books made by the children.
7 Television sets which were either old television cabinets, often easily obtained from dealers, through which children can speak their own programmes; or sets made from boxes through which pictures and captions made by the children were wound on rollers.
8 Washing and ironing materials (educational suppliers produce many delightful washing sets).
9 Window boxes in which children were growing bulbs and plants.

Some schools with plenty of space could put out all their equipment each day for the children to choose from. Where space was more limited, some teachers set out a basic minimum each day and then added equipment for different kinds of activity according to the children's interests on the day of the week, e.g. Monday might be washing day and Friday baking day.

While with the younger children the home area often remains a house, with the older children we found that it might become almost anything. In one school it had, in response to a TV programme, become a castle, with ramparts made from cardboard boxes, where each participant was armed with home-made swords, helmets and shields. Another school had also developed a castle, but here there were guides to show the visitors round, a guide book and teas at the end. Other schools had developed the home area into the hospital, the clinic, the hairdresser's beauty boutique and the fish and chip café. Possibilities seemed almost endless.

In schools where there was no suitable place to set aside as a shop or milk cafeteria, the social area was often arranged to incorporate this in the classroom. There were many ingenious ideas for making educational use of the daily issue of milk. In one middle-class school, where the children went on foreign holidays, there was a central café which was set in a different country each term. Travel posters of the country adorned the walls and the children learned a few phrases of the language needed to order food. In another school the foyer had been turned into an art gallery with the school café in the middle. In classrooms children had made waitress outfits, paid for the milk with plastic or real money, kept accounts and paid the takings into the bank, kept records of those who had drunk milk and the time they had chosen to drink it, sat happily under gay umbrellas or in grottos made from brown paper, clothes horses or boxes.

The social area is also used in many schools for different types of drama. As well as dressing up clothes, some teachers had given much thought to providing stimulating accessories for both girls and boys. Girls seemed particularly to like wigs, beads and brooches, though spectacles (without glass), handbags, gloves and fancy shoes were enjoyed. Boys made good use of some suits of old dress clothes as clowns, ringmasters and waiters, and teachers also found that masks, plastic helmets and false moustaches produced some lively drama as well as the usual fancy ties and bows, belts and hats. Most teachers found that a mirror was essential for the full use of these properties. In some schools where the teacher was interested, part of the social area had been adapted as a puppet theatre, often developed from the Wendy House or a clothes horse. Puppets in general were not elaborate but were made by the children themselves from simple materials such as toilet-roll tubes, clothes pegs, paper bags or rolled-up newspaper, the main objective being to make the characters easily recognizable.

Sets of large building blocks are often provided in schools, as well as construction sets such as Connector or Lego, with which large communal models can be made. One important consideration is to provide a place for building which is out of the path of children moving round the classroom. The teacher in classroom 2 (p. 50) arranges a whole bay for block play with a bookcase at the side on which are stored sets of 'miniature life' material, e.g. zoo animals, farm animals, match-box toys, transport sets, cowboys and Indians and sets of characters that are currently popular on television such as spacemen, footballers, policemen. These help to give a satisfying effect to a constructional project. Other schools put a box of building materials with the building blocks, e.g. hosiery cones, brass and plastic bowls, hair spray tops, cones from trees, wooden slats for ramps, pieces of hardboard for roofs etc.

House play, dramatic activities, cafeteria or shop play and block play seemed to be provided for in the social areas of most schools but, in addition, most teachers provided facilities for other types of social play in response to the children's interests which often arose from watching popular TV programmes.

Science and nature area

Those teachers who were most interested in providing scientific experiences for children stressed that their aim with pupils in the first school was to promote an atmosphere of pleasure and interest in science which would stimulate the children's curiosity and desire to explore their environment. Materials for science, nature study and environmental studies are usually kept in one area of the room, frequently close to the mathematics area since science and mathematics use many tools in common, and children in the integrated day situation are commonly encouraged to take what materials they need from either area and use them in a variety of ways. If the classroom has a sink, the science area is often situated nearby (see p. 50).

Many teachers collect materials for this area for themselves, often helped by the parents and the children who contribute items no longer in use at home — clocks, bells, taps, springs etc. Some schools with parents who work locally in hosiery or engineering firms find them a good source of supply of spare parts, samples of metals, materials etc. The various forms of material collected by the teachers and supplied by the schools seem to be divided into two main categories:

Nonexpendable materials for exploration

1 General equipment for investigation such as magnifying glasses, a microscope, prisms, a thermometer, barometer, magnets and tubes of various kinds. Balancing, weighing and measuring equipment is usually shared with the mathematics area.
2 Heating and lighting equipment such as bulbs, batteries, switches, bells, wire and electricians' screwdrivers. These are sometimes used for illuminating constructional models, dolls' houses and Wendy Houses as well as for simple exploration of their possibilities.
3 Materials for investigating sound such as tuning forks, rattles, drums and tambours with adjustable tension screws (often borrowed from the music area), one-string fiddles and telephones made from string and cans.
4 Materials for investigating the immediate environment include car parts, clocks, irons, kitchen equipment, pulleys, springs.
5 Materials which encourage the investigation of the wider environment such as maps, pictures of the locality, and of scenes known to the children in different weather conditions, and measuring equipment borrowed from the mathematics area.
6 Some children show great interest in accurate charts of the systems of the human body where the teacher has been able to provide these.

Expendable materials for exploration

1 Natural materials such as feathers, fur, wood, stones, cork, shells, fruits, spices etc.
2 Plant life including flowers, vegetables and common weeds which young children often find very pretty.
3 Living things which show the passage of time and seasonal changes and can also be studied for the effects of water, light and dark, heat and cold. These commonly include seeds, fruits, plants, bulbs, saplings grown from seeds.
4 Materials for the comparison of properties which include items which are heavy and light, rough and smooth, thick and thin, transparent and opaque and those which float or sink etc.

Teachers of younger children may find the stimulus of these materials sufficient to start the children exploring and questioning, but we found that with the older children or those in vertically-grouped classes reference books were usually provided. These included the BBC nature pamphlets, picture books, science books written for the age range, and reference books such as the *Junior True* series. Some teachers provided work cards, either written by themselves in response to children's interests or cards made from books, taken to pieces and mounted, that suggested experiments to start the children on rewarding lines of investigation or helped to develop sequential learning from random exploration. Some teachers found boxes of mounted pictures useful. Weather observations, recorded on charts and analysed in various simple ways at stated intervals, or charts on which discoveries about the world of nature or science could be entered up were features of other science areas. In the plan of classroom 1 (p. 49) there are two areas shown for displaying these charts for the children's use. When teachers find that the children are at a stage where they are ready to record their observations and experiments, a table and chairs are often put into the science area or the children are encouraged to use the maths recording area, where it is adjacent and appropriate, to make their records on the various kinds of paper which are provided there. However, sometimes teachers find that the nature record involves writing or drawings, and the work can then be taken to the writing area or the space for creative activities so that some teachers, as in classroom 1, do not provide a special place for science recording.

Children who have made discoveries usually want to show them to others and for this they need display facilities. There were many ways in which teachers provided these, such as:

1 Collections of containers ranging from saucers and yoghurt pots to bulb bowls and vases in which plants could be grown.
2 Collections of containers in which plants could be displayed, e.g. jugs, squeezy bottles with the tops cut off and the printing scrubbed away, painted jam jars, plastic buckets etc.
3 Display stands, sometimes homemade from peg or insulating board, with metal holders for plant pots and clips for specimens in tubes (plastic holders in which tooth brushes are bought make efficient tubes), or sometimes bought ready made from educational suppliers.

In many schools animals were kept as part of the nature programme and the children were often very enthusiastic and communicative about them. There seemed to be two distinct kinds of animal keeping:

1 Animals, which included insects, slugs, caterpillars, snails, millipedes, worms etc which were brought into the class for a short time so that the children could enjoy looking at them quietly.
2 Pets which were intended to remain permanently in the class such as fish, budgerigars, rabbits, gerbils, guinea-pigs, hamsters, stick-insects.

These animals needed suitable homes, many of which were made by teachers and children together, though in the case of birds and fish ready-made cages and aquaria for long-stay pets were usually bought. We found several interesting ideas for containers for animals.

1 Insect cages made from the top and bottom of a large tin, the lid pierced for air holes and the sides extended upwards by a sheet of stiff acetate. An advantage of this insect house is that it is tall enough to take a growing plant or a plant in water on which the insect usually lives (see p. 64).
2 An aquarium made by taking the lid off an old desk and lining it with polythene.
3 Bird feeding and nesting boxes made from polythene containers of varying kinds, from squeezy bottles to the cans in which detergent is sold by the gallon (see p. 64).

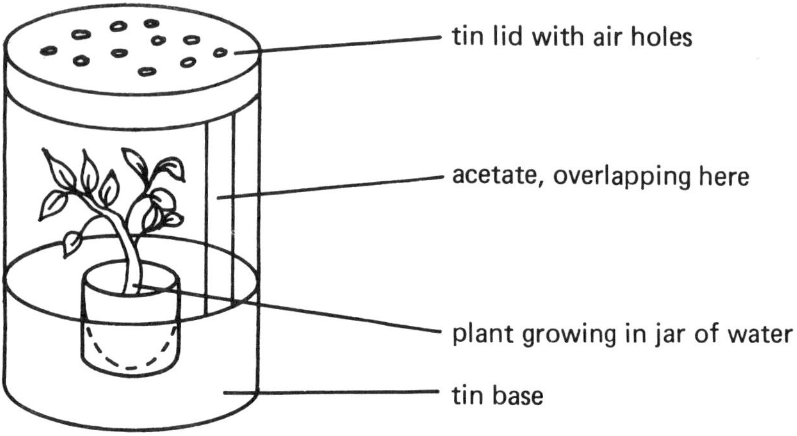

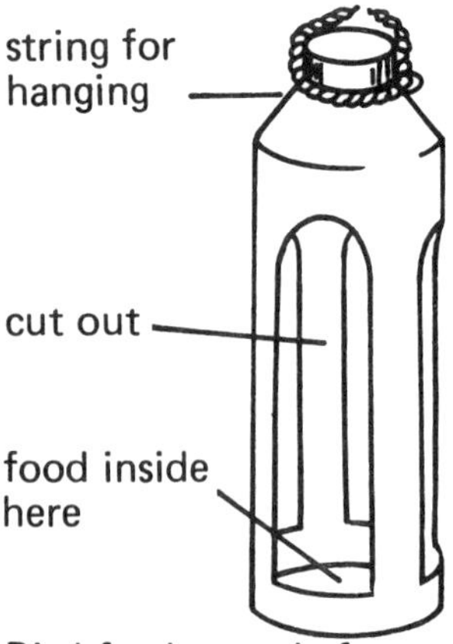

Bird feeder made from plastic bottle

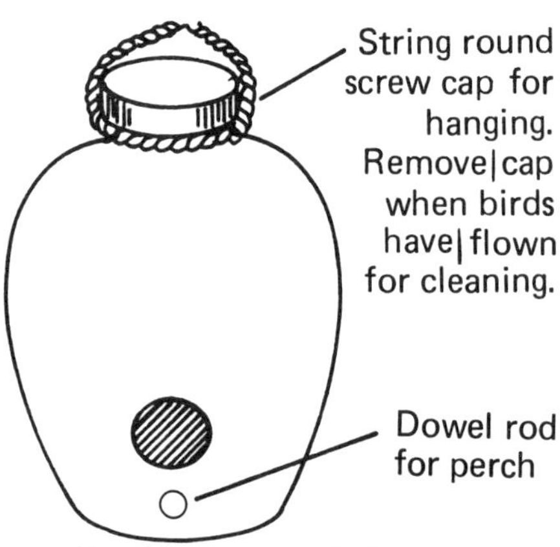

Nesting box made from gallon detergent bottle

4 Wooden box, stained and with a sliding sheet of glass held between two pieces of stripwood, to make a wormery.

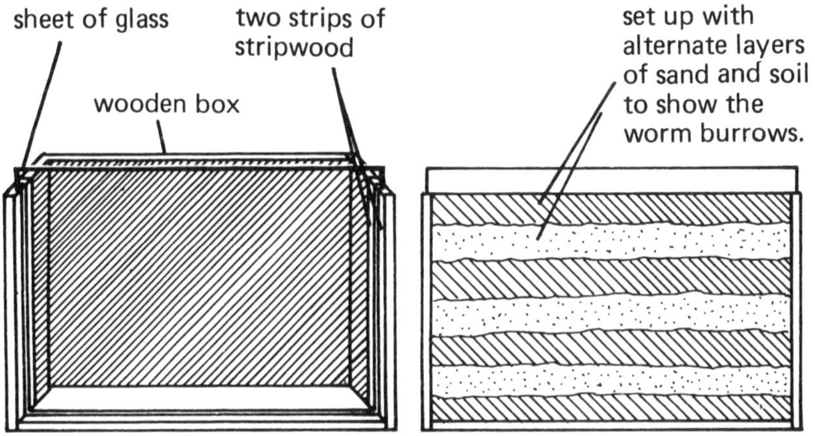

Children seemed to enjoy adapting everyday things to their own use and teachers often felt that the effort required to provide for the needs of growing things enhanced their educational value.

Creative activities area

In all the most modern schools there were special work areas outside the classroom but usually adjoining it and shared by several teachers where all kinds of creative activities could be carried on (see Chapter 2). These areas were usually supplied with sinks, power-points and even water-play alcoves (see p. 27). But in older schools teachers had to adapt suitable parts of the classroom to creative activities, though where a covered verandah was available, or a particularly large assembly hall or foyer, teachers sometimes put selected creative activities there (pp. 43 and 49). The siting of the creative activities area presents special difficulties of noise, movement and equipment which all teachers had to consider and solve in their various ways:

1 Many creative activities (e.g. drawing, embroidery) need particularly good light and may need to be sited near a window, on a glass-roofed verandah, or under an electric light.
2 Many practical activities need water both for the work itself and for clearing up afterwards. If the classroom has a sink, the creative area may be sited near it, though nature and science also need water.

3 Some creative work is by its nature very noisy, for example woodwork and music. In some schools these noisy activities can be put outside the classroom; where this is impossible teachers may decide that they are impractical, or drastically limit the number of children to minimize the noise (perhaps two children only), or make them available only occasionally (one day per week), or while the other children are working at PE etc in the hall (if there is a helper-parent or student who can supervise).

4 Many practical activities need a lot of space. Where space is limited, the teacher may have to consider limiting the number of opportunities she can make available, or set out at any one time only one or two space-hungry activities (modelling, pasting or painting) and add several that take little space (sewing, knitting or weaving on an upright loom etc).

Most schools seemed to provide certain basic equipment:

1 Strong tables for working, floor space for model making, a few chairs where children can sit to do fine work.

2 Protective covering for tables and for floors where necessary. Plastic or rubber sheeting is sometimes available but gardening friends can often supply very large, polythene peat bags which can be split in half and opened out to make strong sheets for covering. Newspaper is usually brought by teachers and children and used when pasting.

3 Protective overalls, often rubber or plastic though some schools have made excellent aprons from old plastic mackintoshes.

4 Large waste bin or basket.

5 Clearing up materials such as dustpans and brush, mop and bucket, floor cloth, dusters, glass cloth, soap and detergent.

Each teacher usually decides for herself which activities are possible with the children from the point of view of space, availability of equipment, children's interests, and her own capacity to supervise and help the children to attain a satisfying standard. Many unusual activities were set up by teachers with special interests but the opportunities most commonly provided seemed to be drawn from the basic half-dozen described below.

Painting, drawing and printing

Some teachers call this the 'image-making' area which provides a clue to the kind of material provided. In their case this is no longer limited to powder paint and large brushes but has branched out to include anything that can be used to construct images, though naturally the basic painting materials are usually presented. Some materials that we have seen include:

1 Painting materials, which are mainly powder paint and various sizes of brushes, including large hog's hair brushes and house painting brushes for the bold worker, small brushes for detailed painting which often intrigues children as their manipulative control increases. Paint is usually mixed ready for younger children and put out in nonspill containers though cut-off squeezy bottles serve the purpose quite well. In many schools older children are taught the elements of colour mixing and mix their own paint in plastic plates, saucers, patty-pan tins. Where brush-holders must be improvised, the funnel of a squeezy bottle holds a brush well if the top third of the bottle is reversed into the bottom third. Some kind of easel is usually provided, although if space is very limited it may only be possible to provide one easel at which two children can work at a time. Some modern schools had long painting boards affixed to walls. These could easily be made.

2 Drawing materials, including various thicknesses of pencil, Biros, coloured Pentel pens and felt pens made from pieces of felt inserted into the ends of dowel rods or short lengths of garden cane, which can be dipped into paint to produce bold lines of varying thicknesses.

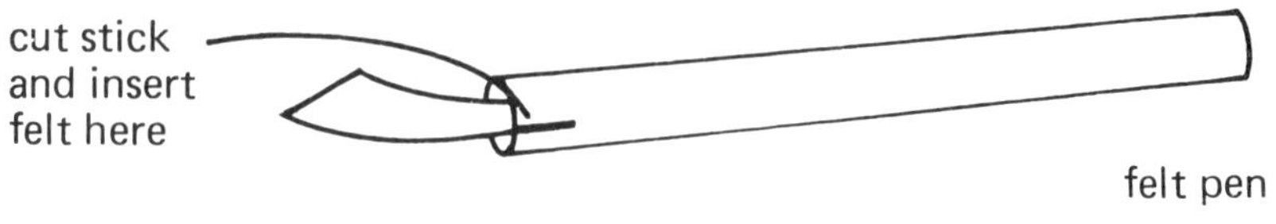

3 Printing materials are very varied and include a large variety of objects for making marks, not forgetting the children's fingers. We have seen children printing with potatoes, onions, string, egg boxes, apples, shells, leaves, Lego parts, bottoms of yoghourt pots, cotton reels, sponges, ends of pencils — the possibilities are endless. Many teachers of young children use powder paint mixed very thick as a printing medium. Some

schools buy tubes of water-based printing ink for the more experienced printers. Some teachers are able to supply small rollers for spreading the printing medium evenly on pieces of Formica, but where this is not possible adequate printing pads can be made from tin lids into which the paint is poured onto layers of cloth or felt.

4 Materials for crayoning usually consisted of various thicknesses of wax crayons which could be used when superimposed for a simple scraper-board technique or, if an electric iron was available to the teacher, for ironing-off prints as well as for the ordinary crayoning that many children enjoy and for wax-resist painting.

5 Papers of various colours, textures and sizes varying from the very large to the small, particularly with the older children who pass through a stage of wanting to draw in more detail as an exploitation of their growing manual dexterity. Very young children are often content to paint on newspaper and some teachers find it a stimulating material for older children too.

6 A variety of materials for exploitation of paints and papers — scissors, straws for blowing, combs, stiff brushes such as plastic nail brushes and Vim, sand or sawdust to texture paint etc.

Model making and pasting

We found that in the infant or first school this was largely based on a copious and marvellous supply of *junk*. If there is space only for one junk-box, it may contain every possible shape of box and many different sizes, hosiery cones and spools, bobbins and cotton reels, toilet-rolls and kitchen paper tubes, egg boxes, papier-maché trays which once held meat or fish in a supermarket deep freeze, lengths of polystyrene. Where more space is available, materials are often sorted into various containers. In addition most teachers provide smaller containers into which small materials such as beads, sequins, macaroni, haricot and butter beans, feathers, buttons, matchsticks, artificial flowers, coloured sweetpapers etc can be sorted.

In addition to this basic junk, schools usually seemed to provide:

1 A wide variety of different colours and textures of paper, e.g. newspaper, old wallpaper books, wrapping paper, tissue paper, crêpe paper, paper doyleys, and corrugated papers from chocolate boxes and corrugated cardboard. Some teachers rationed the rarer or more expensive papers or kept them for

the older, abler children. In many schools picture papers and magazines were available for paper collage.

2 Cloth remnants of various kinds, a variety of thicknesses and textures of string, pieces of fur, balls of wool, felt offcuts.

3 A variety of pastes and glues so that the one most appropriate for the job can be selected, either by the teacher of the younger children or by the older children themselves. Paste brushes in a variety of sizes and containers for paste such as cream or yoghourt cartons. Containers such as tin lids for glue where it is not provided in tubes. A supply of cleaning rags and whatever cleaning agent will remove particular kinds of glues from children's fingers.

4 Scissors which can be stored in a slotted tray or cardboard box, points downwards, and also rulers and set squares.

If space allows, many teachers provide two modelling tables, one for constructing the model and the other as a pasting or gluing table for this helps to prevent unwanted adhesives from other models getting onto a child's work.

Plastic modelling area

The most common modelling materials that we saw provided for plastic modelling were clay, papier mâché, flour and salt mixture while some schools still use Plasticine. Block salt is used for sculpture where teachers are able to obtain it.

Clay

Experienced teachers suggest that if the claybin is lined with polythene, the clay rolled into balls of reasonable size, and the thumb pressed into the ball to make a cavity which is then filled with water before being wrapped in polythene, the clay will remain at a good modelling consistency for a long time. It is usual to provide each child with a clay board or tile to work on, and a container of water together with a piece of sponge or rag with which he can keep his model damp and his fingers clean. Often teachers supply a box of tools for firming, beating, pressing and incising such as modelling tools, rolling pin, pieces of wire and twig, matchsticks, bottle tops, flat pieces of wood, a fairly blunt kitchen knife, string, rope, shells, seeds etc. A supply of plastic bags is useful for wrapping unfinished work to keep it damp. We found a variety of ways in which children were able to finish their work when dried.

1 Where the school had a kiln or shared a kiln with the junior or middle school, the best work was fired and sometimes glazed.
2 Models worth preserving were painted and then varnished with a paper varnish.
3 Candle ends were used for waxing clay surfaces where the models had been fired once but not glazed.
4 In conjunction with children in the junior or middle school, teachers sometimes build an experimental kiln in the school grounds.

Plasticine

The materials supplied to the children seem to be much the same as those needed for clay work, except that the Plasticine is usually kept in a tin and, of course, needs no damping or finishing.

Papier mâché

Teachers seem to supply a variety of materials for making this modelling material such as newspaper, egg boxes, deep freeze trays, and used sugar paper, the main consideration being an absence of 'dressing' in the material. If these substances are torn up, put in a bucket of cold-water paste and water mixed according to the directions on the packet, soaked for several days and then beaten up with the end of a rolling pin, an adequate modelling material seems to be obtained. It is often kept in balls in a polythene bucket and covered with a piece of plastic. It can be modelled on a board or tile, dried in the sun or over the radiator and then painted and varnished, so that teachers often find that the tools supplied for clay modelling are also used by the children for papier mâché.

Flour and salt

The recipe commonly used is given on page 58. This material, once made up, can be stored for a week in plastic bags in a large tin or polythene container. It is particularly useful for making beads which can be dried on knitting needles or lengths of wire, or for making small models of people and animals. If sets of patty-pans are provided, play cakes and tarts for shops and Wendy Houses can be made. This material sets rock hard and can be painted.

Plastic modelling usually needs to be done on a strong, firm table so that the children can beat, press or wedge their clay and papier mâché. The table is best covered with some waterproof material such as plastic or rubber sheeting, but where money is short, table covers have been made from old plastic raincoats cut to size and tied with tape to the table legs. Protective covering for the floor may be necessary if the children are being very messy but newspaper often provides quite adequate protection.

Woodwork area

There are many schools fortunate enough to possess a woodwork bench and a supply of appropriate tools such as hammers, pliers, pincers, tin-snips, tenon-saws and surform-boards, while some children are lucky in having tool-conscious parents to aid and guide them. Where it is in line with school policy, such parents can come into school to help small groups of children at stated times. If no bench is available, interested teachers have used a stout wooden table with a bench hook for each child carpenter, usually two or four at a time. Many schools provide a tool rack, often made from pegboard with silhouettes of the tools painted in their appropriate places and hooks to hang them on, or holes can be made at the ends of woodwork benches and the tools hung in the slots. Children also need both oval and round nails of different lengths sorted into containers such as yoghourt pots or jam jars, and sandpaper of various thicknesses.

Teachers have found that children produce better models if supplied with lengths and pieces of planed and square wood than when given old boxes to break up. Sources of scrap wood tapped by teachers include:

1 The undertaker.
2 The local carpenter and handyman.
3 Building firms, either at the main works or on a particular building site.
4 Furniture-making firms.
5 The local boat-builder.

These sources have been found most helpful in supplying free to teachers small, interesting, nicely finished and shaped bits of scrap wood if the teacher pays a weekly visit and leaves a large cardboard box into which the workmen can throw scraps as they work. Wheels can be sawn from lengths of broom handle, though usually teachers have found that they have had to prepare a supply of these for the children. In general, this is an activity usually reserved for the older children in the school who have reached the stage when they are beginning to want to acquire skill and are getting some strength in their hands.

Work with textiles

In schools for young children this work seems mainly to consist of sewing (which includes embroidery and collage, as well as the beginnings of needlework), knitting and weaving.

Sewing

The materials provided usually include some of the following:

1 A variety of materials for making small articles and dolls' clothes, and to form backgrounds for collage, e.g. felt, binca cloth, checked and striped gingham, all of which lend themselves to embroidery as well.
2 A collection of sewing cottons, embroidery threads and coloured wools.
3 Materials for collage, e.g. pieces of cotton, wool and silk fabrics, lace, ribbon, tape, sequins, beads, feathers, seeds, string, raffia etc.
4 Tools for sewing, such as thimbles, sharp scissors, pinking shears, pins and needles which have large eyes so that the children can thread them. Some teachers of young children keep a supply of ready-threaded needles in a pincushion or a piece of material. Crewel needles are useful for embroidery and Copydex for sticking pieces of collage in position.
5 Older children seemed to appreciate patterns of rag dolls, stuffed animals, dolls' clothes where these were provided, while younger children enjoyed sewing cards, often drawn by themselves round templates and pricked by the teacher.

Knitting

Materials for beginners are simple and children in the first school rarely attain sufficient skill or have sufficient patience to complete anything large or intricate. Schools that teach knitting seem to provide:

1 Yarn or four-ply wool in small balls and attractive shades. If the balls tend to roll around, some teachers let the children keep them in tins or jam jars while knitting.
2 Short needles suitable for children's hands; size 8 seems to be appropriate for beginners.

3 With older children knitting patterns devised by the teacher and often drawn on squared paper are popular and sometimes lead on to children devising their own.

Weaving

Most schools provided a commercially-produced card frame which is comparatively cheap and had the advantage of being accurately marked out. With this a large-size weaving needle with a long pointed end was used. Various experimental forms of weaving were being used in a few schools:

1 A weaving frame for beginners. Brass-headed carpet tacks were hammered into an old picture frame and curtain rings sewn onto both ends of appropriate lengths of braid. The child's task was first to set up a warp by putting the rings over the tacks and then weave the lengths of braid across it. This was a piece of learning equipment, and at the end the child returned the braids to the box ready for the next learner.

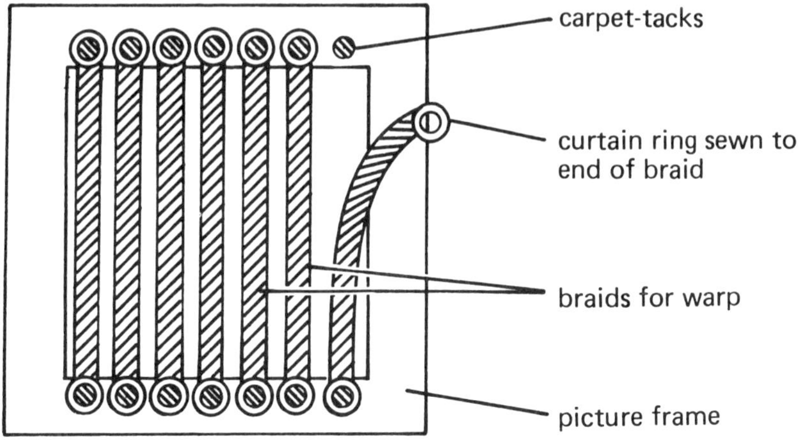

2 Use of string warps nailed to large boards for making rugs as a class effort. The weft was made in one school from rug wool and in another from strips of nylon stocking.

3 Paper weaving used for inventing patterns, where the teacher cut the 'looms' from squared or lined paper with a razor blade or Stanley knife, and the children weave with paper strips.

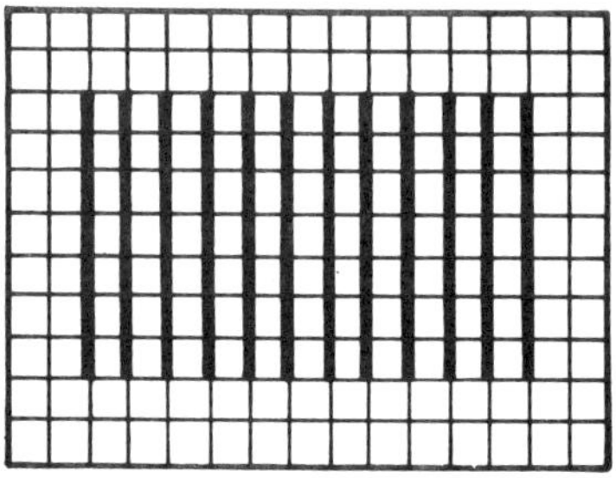

'loom' cut in squared paper

Sand and water

These activities were provided in almost every class though their extent varied according to available space and storage. In general, two lines of approach were noticed, some teachers providing for one, some for the other and a few for both.

1 The investigatory approach or 'what can we do with sand?' Wherever possible teachers provided both wet and dry sand, sometimes simultaneously but, where space was limited, on different days so that their varying qualities could be explored and sometimes only in very small trays. To assist exploration of both water and sand, a variety of tools was provided, e.g. buckets, spades, rubber tubing, sieves, plastic mugs and jugs with and without holes in the bottom, plastic bottles, potato mashers, squeezy bottles.

2 The imaginative approach where materials were available for building-up imaginary scenes, e.g. sets of miniature life models, animals, fish, transport models including ships, trees or materials for representing trees such as cones, twigs, pieces of evergreen. Small blocks for building seemed to be well used where provided and one or two schools had sets of heavy stone blocks with which harbours and underwater caves or palaces could be built.

In one school the children's interest in water had encouraged them to build their own fish pond, and other schools gave children experiences of blowing soap bubbles, changing water in the aquarium by syphoning, watering plants through various sizes of rose on watering cans, etc.

Books and pictures

We found that most teachers who were successful in stimulating their children to a high degree of creativity provided and discussed not only materials in the creative activity area, but also books and pictures which suggested how to use the materials in new ways or find and use other materials. Some teachers brought in interesting things that had been found on holiday or made by themselves which they thought would give the children a lead, and in many cases children were also able to bring such things from home.

Music

Wherever children are given the opportunity to experiment with sounds and to make music for themselves, there is the problem of the level of sound rising as the children are playing the instruments, while they also need quiet for listening. In many schools the musical activities take place in the school hall or in any other secluded spot, but in other schools the music area must perforce remain in the classroom. This is not impossible though the scope of the instruments provided, particularly the percussion, will obviously be limited.

In the classroom we found rather different provision for younger and older children. Younger children were largely experimenting with sound and rhythm and much of the equipment was home-made:

1 Plastic bottles partly filled with sand, and with various kinds and sizes of seeds to make shakers which would give a variety of sounds.
2 Milk bottle tops threaded on wire twisted into a circle for shakers.
3 Short lengths of dowell-rod for rhythm sticks.
4 Bells threaded on ribbon.
5 Wooden beads threaded on separate strands and then woven into a band so that they 'clacked' together.
6 An up-turned plastic bowl made a drum.
7 Saucepan lids for make-shift cymbals.

However, some instruments should be bought as they are extremely difficult to make accurately, e.g. glockenspiels, harps, pipes, castanets, xylophones.

With older children the equipment is often increased and some definite plan of arranging the music area helps the children to select and put away instruments easily. There is often shelving or a bookcase for storing recorders, clappers, shakers, bells, cymbals, sticks and drums unless these are mounted on stands. A flat surface of some kind, such as a wider shelf screwed to the bookcase or a special table, is usually provided to hold glockenspiels, xylophones, harps and violindas. Some schools have both metal and wooden glockenspiels; many teachers show the children how to make and tune a glockenspiel made from a row of bottles containing varying depths of water, strung in a row to make a scale.

The music area may also include a tape recorder or record player, with or without earphones, to encourage the children to record their own tunes and listen to the tunes of others. Some teachers gave older children materials for making written records, e.g. writing and drawing materials and music paper, and also music books and song books suitable for their stage of musical development.

While it is possible for the interested teacher to have a music area in the classroom if no other alternative exists, it is obviously more practical, and certainly cheaper, to have all the instruments in the central hall or one place in the corridor where they will be available to a large number of children and will not need to be duplicated. Schools who organize in this way find they have to plan very carefully to see that all children have a fair time in the music area, and may accommodate groups from one class on each day for short sessions so that all children use the area each week.

One such music area was arranged at one end of the main hall of a ten-class infant school. It consisted of a flat surface against the wall, flanked by side shelves with the piano nearby. A stand supported the drum and a further pair of supports held the bottle glockenspiels, strung on brightly coloured cord. A large, upturned wooden box, gaily painted by the children, lay on the floor as a second drum. At the back of the piano keyboard were pasted the names of the notes and some elementary piano music was available on the side shelves which also held music books, drawing-paper, crayons and felt-tipped pens for recording. Prominently displayed was a felt contact board and a box containing felt letters, crochets and quavers etc. The rest of the shelves held a variety of instruments. There was also a tape recorder for the children to use in recording their music. This music area was in general supervised by the head, though groups were often left here to continue their music-making by themselves, and some of the teachers in the school followed up the work by having groups of instruments also available in their classrooms.

The children's use of work areas

Work areas are arranged mainly to fulfil three functions:

1 to stimulate and develop the children's interests
2 to house the equipment necessary for covering particular fields of study
3 to provide working space.

However, experienced teachers find that as children develop an interest, the field of study may move from one work area to another. For instance, a group that is making music in the music area may become fascinated by the relationship between pitch and the length of xylophone bar or violinda string and to investigate this further may need the equipment that is kept in the science area. They may wish to make a dance or play to accompany their tunes and either move to the drama section or borrow material from it. They may need to use the creative activities area to paint a picture of their music. Teachers seem to deal with this need for fluidity in one of two ways. Either the child or the group transfers to the area which contains the equipment needed or, if this area is already filled with working children, they can borrow the equipment needed and take it to where they are working. In some cases both the required area and the equipment are being used by others and the children have to learn to put their problem by for a little and return to it at an appropriate time.

Chapter 4

THE ROLE OF THE HEADTEACHER

There are probably as many varieties of the integrated day as there are teachers practising it. Considerable variation in ways of organizing work may operate in any one school and this presents problems for the headteacher who has the task of 'integrating' the teachers. The role of the headteacher may therefore be seen as involving a fundamental dichotomy. The head who believes in the integrated day is likely to believe that one of the main aims of education is the optimum development of the individual in society, which applies to teachers no less than to children. At the same time, the headteacher is *ex officio* responsible for the organization and standards of the whole school. In *Standards and Progress in Reading* (Morris 1966) the investigators state: 'After the attributes of their population and material conditions had been considered, each school's success or failure in promoting good reading standards and/or progress seemed to depend primarily on the quality of the head.'

Headteachers are therefore faced with the task of providing for various interpretations of the integrated day, based on the individual understanding, temperament and classroom situation of each teacher, while at the same time protecting the well-being, happiness and development of every child in their care.

Preparation for reorganization as an integrated day school

There are many cases where a school has been working successfully with a formal organization but the headteacher wishes to reorganize on an integrated basis, either because she is beginning to question the value of formal methods or because she comes as a new head from an integrated school. Heads who have reorganized their schools stress the importance of making haste slowly, taking plenty of time to consider, carefully thinking out ideas and collecting information before initiating discussions with the staff. They suggest that the head who wishes to introduce the integrated day may profitably refresh her mind by reading such relevant books as are available, and then practise marshalling her arguments by discussion with other headteachers and local authority advisors. Most have found it helpful to visit other schools which already operate a successful integrated day, so that many varied schemes may be seen in practice and discussed with heads and teaching staffs. In some cases, they have found it necessary to obtain permission to visit schools in other local authority areas. Most heads who already operate the integrated day are convinced of the need for individual thought, and say that the head who is likely to run a successfully integrated school is one who does not 'jump on the bandwaggon' but calmly thinks out a system that she feels will be appropriate to her own children, staff and school buildings, bearing in mind the personalities and temperaments of her teachers. There is also the question of the needs of the children in the particular school and a decision to be reached on how controlled their integrated day will need to be in the beginning. Freedom is alarming and a considerable responsibility. Not many children, and very few teachers, can tolerate too much freedom if given suddenly.

When the headteacher has cleared her own mind, she will commonly approach the staff. She can do this in two ways: either she can present her plan and try to sell it to her teachers; or she can present the general principles of integration as material for discussion, and try to get the teachers themselves to put forward ideas for implementing these principles, using her own plan mainly to keep her mind clear, and to offer as her contribution to the general fund of ideas. It depends on the head's concepts of authority and democracy, and on the general tone of the staff, as well as the amount of time available for discussion, which plan the head adopts. There is no doubt that the second plan, while more democratic and creative, is far more time-consuming than the first. In any case, it is usually advisable first to approach the deputy head and possibly other senior teachers, for if their support is enlisted, the most important step has been taken.

First, there must be plenty of time for informal discussion in the staffroom. Heads who have already taken this step suggest that there should be no feeling of undue haste but that a general climate of discussion of different methods of organization should be initiated. Some heads provide a staff library of relevant books, perhaps by making their own available, requisitioning others and borrowing from local and professional libraries. Some local librarians will organize block issues of books to schools on particular topics such as the integrated day if the head can supply a booklist. Publishers will send inspection copies or organize displays of books if sufficient time is allowed. Colleges of education, university schools of education and local advisors are often helpful in the compilation of booklists. If there are teachers on the staff who have previously worked an integrated day, they may be able to offer advice on books.

Many heads make it possible for teachers to visit schools where they can see the integrated day in action. After a visit, a definite staff conference can be arranged when a report is given to the rest of the teachers, followed by a discussion. These conferences can take place in the lunch break or after school. Heads who have regular staff meetings as a normal part of school routine are in an advantageous position here, for their teachers are accustomed to organizing life to include a late session in school, or a regular lunch-time meeting at stated intervals.

This stage of planning usually ends when some general agreement is reached on how the change should begin. It may be agreed that there should be a trial period of several weeks by a few teachers, as a pilot experiment. The headteacher might perhaps ask for volunteers, giving time for thought but at the same time building up confidence all round by expressing with her appreciation of what the staff is already doing and noting the degree of integration already attained. As the teachers who volunteer to start the integrated day will later be a valuable source of reference for the others, the headteacher may well feel it advisable to concentrate on helping them with their problems, supporting them in their difficulties and showing lively appreciation of their successes.

It may, however, be agreed that the changeover should be begun simultaneously in all classes. Either way, the staff is likely to agree on a date by which the school as a whole will change to the integrated day. If there are convinced antiintegrationists on the staff, the policy of many heads is to leave them for a time since they are more likely to be won over by example than by argument. There is much truth in the saying, 'A man convinced against his will, Is of the same opinion still,' and one can find schools where the head has insisted on integration throughout and the dissident teachers seize every opportunity to return to formal teaching disguised in various ways as freedom.

There seem to be two varieties of anti-integrationist teacher.

One holds perfectly genuine views that the integrated day is not in the children's best interests. She is a teacher who has read and thought, but this is her considered opinion. In such cases, the head may like to remember that difference of opinion may act as a yeast in the dough of conformity, continually forcing the integrating teachers to explain and justify themselves. Difference can provide stimulus and provoke clarity of thought. Teachers, moreover, tend to teach best by whatever method they personally feel right. The realization of the validity of individual differences is perhaps an important part of the education of both teachers and children. These teachers may be making a genuine contribution by dissenting and, in any case, may be best left to teach in their own way.

There are other teachers who, often unknown to themselves, are anti-integrationists through inertia or fear. These are more likely to be won over by example. Possibly the head may employ a successful integrated day convert to show tactfully how it can be done. The head may continually encourage these teachers, boost their morale, praise their efforts, however slight, and persuade them that she has thought long and hard, that she is convinced that the change is right and necessary, and that she and the more experienced teachers will support them at every stage.

Preparation of the rooms and equipment is a further step. The headteacher is the only member of staff with an overall picture of the school, so with her lies the responsibility of arranging the fair distribution of furniture and equipment. She may need also to requisition some additional apparatus and equipment, particularly small apparatus for mathematics, games, puzzles, construction toys, bricks, all to be kept in hand ready for the starting date. Some headteachers ask each teacher to make a list of the equipment and the furniture she feels she will need. She then collates these lists and apportions both old and new material as fairly as possible, some to each teacher's stock room, some to the children's shelves, and the large items that all must share to the central store. Some heads emphasize the need to ensure enough equipment in each room, not merely for present needs but for progression. Many heads, together with the class teacher, take stock of each room, deciding which furniture should be thrown out and also where it should be put. Indeed, it is the task of the head in her own individual way to mobilize the resources of the whole school building to serve the integrated day. A problem common in all schools is the delineation of the quiet areas of the school, where children may consult books or sit and think. The opportunity for privacy is highly important. Some heads make use of every alcove, the passages, the entrance hall and the medical room to provide places for small groups or for individuals. Environmental influences on children are subtle and highly important and many a head finds an enjoyable challenge in surveying the school, planning so that the effect is exciting and visually attractive, deciding where she will arrange her own displays for the benefit of the whole school, and where she can show children's work. Before the integrated day starts, it is helpful to begin collecting such materials which will help make displays attractive, e.g. old picture frames, lengths of cloth of varying textures and colours, well-shaped pottery, unusual papers and boxes.

All this time the vitally important preparation of the children will be progressing. Some school staffs hold meetings to discuss and agree on their priorities for the next few weeks with regard to the attitudes to be developed in the children. Before an integrated day has any real chance of success, the children must start to acquire a degree of *self*-discipline and independence. Heads may feel a need to discuss and come to an agreement with their staff on how various forms of school organization can be rearranged to encourage these objectives, e.g. how the children are now to be trained to enter and leave the building and the assembly hall; how and when they are to use cloakrooms, toilets, outside play spaces and facilities; the organization needed for morning milk, school dinners, money for shopping activities etc. Where the school has previously been rather formal, parts of the school day may need considerable reappraisement if the children are to acquire individual responsibility.

As plans for the changeover become settled, many heads feel it is time to begin to take the parents into their confidence, so that they will understand the reasons for the change and the exact changes that are proposed. By organizing information sessions for parents, most heads become certain of a measure of support and where parents disagree with the new policy, at least a degree of tolerance is possible. They often find that the more interested parents are in the children's education, the more likely they are to worry about the effect of innovation on the child's academic attainment and the more they will value explanation, reassurance and a chance to put questions. It is also possible that children may be upset by the change and need parental understanding.

There are four main ways in which headteachers have been known to organize this explanation to the parents. If there is already a Parent-Teacher Association a series of meetings can be arranged. It may be advisable to hold at least two, and possibly more, meetings to provide an opportunity for the headteacher first to explain what is happening and then allow plenty of time for an initial rush of questions and criticisms. She might wish to follow this up by some form of practical demonstration such as another meeting where a film is shown and discussed. Another possibility tried in some schools is an evening with a guest speaker, such as the local advisor or inspector, or a 'Brains Trust' consisting of heads of schools which already work an integrated day.

There might be a final meeting where small discussion groups are organized, each led by a member of the school staff. Such a series of meetings can, of course, be organized where there is no PTA but is rather less easy to arrange than where there is established custom.

Sometimes headteachers have invited small groups of parents to visit the school at the end of the afternoon so that they can explain their plans and talk to them over a cup of tea. In such cases, the parents at each session have usually been drawn from the children of one class, so that the class teacher, as well as the deputy head, can be present. This method is more time consuming but has been found to have the advantage that discussion groups can be kept small so that all may have a chance to ask questions. In the large PTA meeting, it is often the same parents who take the lead while more diffident members fail to make themselves heard, but the afternoon group has the disadvantage that too many fathers are at work in the afternoon and cannot attend. In some areas, however, it is possible to arrange these sessions for the evening with a strong likelihood that most parents will manage to come and headteachers, knowing their districts, will be aware of which course is most likely to succeed in their own catchment area.

Other heads prepare a cyclostyled booklet, often in addition to arranging meetings. This has three advantages; it makes misrepresentation of what the head has said rather more difficult; it acts as a later reference handbook for the use of parents; it is available for those parents who were unable to attend meetings.

When matters have been set in motion with the teachers, the children and the parents, a definite date can be published for the changeover. Many heads try to arrange extra time for the teachers to make the additional apparatus, assignment cards and other equipment that they will need, although others require their staff to do this extra work at home in the evenings or in the vacation.

Some heads adopt ingenious methods for giving their teachers extra free time. Where the school is used by colleges of education, the preparation for the changeover can take place during second or third teaching practice, for where students are reasonably competent they usually welcome chances to be alone with the classes while the teachers work in the staffroom or utility room. Headteachers may also organize their own work so that in rotation they are able to release a teacher for a whole day and take over her class. One headteacher of a junior school took sole responsibility for her whole school in the assembly hall for a week, while the teachers prepared materials in the classrooms (we do not exactly recommend this as a practical form of organization for others).

When all is prepared, the great day arrives. There are bound to be feelings of both excitement and apprehension which many heads try to contain by deliberately playing a calming and supporting role, whatever their own feelings. As a wise headmistress put it, 'My advice to a head during the changeover is, "Be brave! Have confidence in one's own ability! Have faith in one's ideals".'

The implementation

Once the changeover has taken place, experienced heads suggest that the main work lies in maintaining the confidence of the teachers by being willing to begin slowly, realizing that it may take several years for a really good integrated day pattern to become established throughout the school. It is important for the headteacher to use the positive rather than the negative side of her personality; she must never undermine the confidence of the staff but rather show pleasure and approval at the individual efforts of the teachers to fit into a way of working which may mean much extra work for them. Some might perhaps call this positive aspect 'insincere' and of course this will be true if the head does not genuinely feel approval and appreciation, but most heads of integrated schools seem to us to have a genuine admiration for much of their teachers' work which they have only to allow themselves to express.

Many headteachers recommend spending as much time as possible out and about in the school with the aim of visiting each classroom once every day and being seen constantly around the school. This enables them to keep a careful eye on teachers' morale and also to help realistically with teaching, working with the teacher to get the integrated day pattern established. The need for the discussion of problems will now be greatly increased and the head may really need to spend some coffee or lunch breaks in the staffroom, encouraging teachers to talk about their work and how it is developing, and to see where they can help each other. Teachers can be encouraged to move from their own areas to visit other classrooms, either to help by using their specialist knowledge or to see how another teacher copes with a problem that they themselves find difficult.

The need for organization and planning for the day or the week and thinking ahead for the possible progression of work for the whole term may now be realized. Some headteachers find it useful to ask their staff to hand in forecasts of work for the week or the month, to clear the teachers' minds and keep the head in touch with developments. Many heads have seen particular need at some time to remind the staff that integration does not mean 'licence' and that good academic progress is essential. They know that valuable as individual work and group activities are, there is still room for the class lesson and a need to 'teach' and stretch the children: the 'integrated day' is not the 'do-exactly-as-you-please day'. This delicate balance between teaching and learning is very difficult to adjust and the head might find a need to give much help here, as teachers err on the side of too much teaching or too much laissez-faire.

In addition to asking for forecasts of work to be done, or as in some schools instead of requiring forecasts, heads frequently initiate and insist upon careful record keeping, considering this absolutely essential to effective work. Indeed, we find it difficult to see how a successful integrated day can be run without systematic and detailed record keeping (this point is discussed further in Chapter 9). Sometimes the head and the staff together work out record forms suitable for the particular school. In other schools each teacher is encouraged to work out her own but the records are seen by the head at stated intervals and approved by her. These records might form a basis for discussion between the head and the class teacher and provide some of the material for staff meetings. Experienced teachers have suggested that it helps the integration and cross-fertilization of their work where the head arranges to hold regular staff meetings. If they know that meetings are scheduled for regular times, such as the first Wednesday in the month, 3.30–5.00, and if the head also takes care that the time is never exceeded, they often welcome the chance to discuss their experiences and seldom object to staying late. Teachers accustomed to such meetings feel strongly that it is essential for the head to chair such meetings *firmly*, so that they are constructive, and not mere 'grumble sessions'. Discussion they feel should be kept to the point and not allowed to become simply anecdotal; every teacher's opinion should be invited; no one person and no one group should be allowed to dominate the meeting. At the end of the meeting, some definite conclusion should be reached if possible so that the staff go away with the feeling of a job well done rather than with a sense of futility.

Once the early classroom problems are solved, pressure of numbers in the classroom may be eased by organizing activities in areas of the school other than classrooms, where the headteacher might wish to work with children, possibly with help from students or parents, on interests of her own. There are schools where the head is responsible for all the music or the science in the school, and gathers all the equipment together in the hall, where at stated times interested children come to work with her. In addition heads usually wish to keep an eye on the general equipment, seeing that it is kept flowing and used to the best advantage. Busy teachers may forget to return equipment to the central store, so that it can be almost forgotten and pass out of use.

It seems that many heads of integrated day schools find that their main duty at this stage is to appear calm and confident, to give liberal encouragement and appreciation to their staff and to be seen actively working and teaching in the school. They stress, however, that appreciation should be genuine and based on the development of positive attitudes towards the work of their teachers, otherwise it may be felt as a hypocritical 'pill-sweetener' or 'donkey-carrot'. It is as possible to establish a mental 'set' towards appreciation as it is towards blame but it is not, perhaps, so common in our culture.

The continued working of the integrated day

Once the integrated day is established the pattern of the headteacher's work seems to change. Many heads told us that they needed continually to reassess themselves. They stress the importance of guarding against complacency and the feeling that, because integration has begun, one is 'there'. One is never 'there', they say. In teaching there is never an equilibrium on which one can rest but merely a balance of many opposing forces to which adjustment must continually be made. As suggested earlier, all heads are faced with dichotomy in their dealings with the staff.

They have to face up to what, in the words of Susan Isaacs, must be regarded as a 'permanent impermanence'. Experienced teachers know that what works on Monday is quite likely not to work on Thursday, that what suits Mrs Smith may be useless for Miss Jones and that what suits Group A may be quite unrealistic with Group B. The headteacher's role is therefore seen by some heads as consciously to try to remain self-critical, alert, detached and, as far as possible, healthy since the integrated day will make great demands on her vitality and time.

Perhaps the most important part of her contribution will be the active support and encouragement that she gives to her teachers. Many heads continue to visit classrooms regularly, showing their genuine interest in what is going on, admiring that which is good but being ready to meet that which is not with a constructive suggestion. Classroom visits can provide that second opinion, another person who may see things in a new light and may send a project off on a fresh line of enquiry, or suggest a new way of looking at a problem. Teachers often say that they like to feel that the head is available to discuss with individuals their ideas, problems and the development of their work. They find these discussions helpful and stimulating. They appreciate heads who are ready to show how suggestions can be carried out by actually teaching a group or taking a class when the teacher is at a loss.

Although an integrated day is working it may still not necessarily be of the best quality. By quality, we mean not merely something done but the amount of knowledge and reflective thought behind what is done. It may be necessary to organize or stimulate general discussions of policy, the philosophy behind the school organization and attitudes to teaching, the fundamental educational ideas that underlie the selection of material for the children. As far as possible, every aspect of school life should be kept open to question and revision, and heads may wish their teachers to attend courses and exhibitions to provide material for intelligent discussion and be willing to go with them. A few heads, however, mention the importance of recognizing that the bow cannot always be kept bent and that educational topics tend, perhaps, to become over-absorbing for conscientious teachers. While vacation courses are stimulating, real holidays are important for securing emotional balance and elasticity of mind.

There is also the question of how to pass on to teachers any new ideas that may come from the advisory staff, inspectors, colleges of education or from the head's own reading. Heads who in some way share their reading with their staffs, who bring books into school for use, display and discussion, seem to set a pattern for their teachers which in time improves their professional ability. Some find that offering of a book personally to an individual teacher is successful, for example 'I thought you might like to read this book Mrs Smith, before I take it back to the library; it is right on your line of interest about reading difficulties.' Other heads recommend a book in a general way while some require teachers to read and discuss new publications. There are heads who draw the attention of teachers to stimulating television or radio programmes on educational or social topics and initiate informal discussions afterwards.

Since the head is moving continually round her school, she is the teacher who is best able to see the school environment in its totality and provide for the children's needs where these cannot be catered for in classrooms or by her staff. In the first place, organizing a room for integrated work needs much planning and takes time and most heads help their teachers with suggestions or materials as required, encouraging them to feel proud of their rooms and their achievements. Interesting work may be selected by the head and put on display for the benefit of the whole school. If it is possible to set up the display in the entrance hall, visiting parents can also see the work and gain more insight into the school. Often parents who see such a display can contribute something themselves which draws them into a closer relationship with the school. Such displays of group work may also arouse such interest that they can be extended to include the whole school. School assemblies may provide an opportunity to talk to pupils and teachers about these displays and bring their work together. In some schools, the head allots certain assemblies to each class for displaying and explaining their work. Sometimes these displays are organized round a theme. For instance, harvest time can be an occasion for bringing together and showing the work of various groups on the harvesting of grain, fruit, and vegetables; on seeds and how they are spread, used and stored; on the making of flour and bread; on harvesting in art, poetry, song and story. The more that the work of individual children or groups can be drawn together, the more community feeling will be generated in the school and this may be considered one of the functions of the headteacher, though class teachers will often make suggestions which she can follow up.

Many heads will also wish to arrange displays of their own. As they are working around the various rooms, they can often pinpoint the material which would just highlight or encourage a certain interest or investigation. The head is conversant with the school's resources of visual aids, charts, pictures, collections of things to see and handle including the range of available junk material. She is in a position to arrange displays of new materials so that all can see what is available and be stimulated to use it. She can also put on show materials which she feels are being neglected, together with books or written captions that might spark off ideas. Some heads make themselves responsible for areas where the whole staff is deficient — often science or music. The head herself may be equally deficient but may make it her business to study the work available in this field and try to provide some suitable experiences for the children. Where the head has the taste and ability, she may wish to be responsible for the beauty of the child's school environment by arranging exhibitions of pictures, objects and lovely colours. If she is talented in flower arranging, this can be her interest and responsibility. But if she is not endowed with an eye for decoration, it would be helpful if she could find a substitute and organize time for her to make the school a place of beauty as well as interest.

A resource department is a project for the headteacher that will prove of great benefit to her staff. Many offices and firms produce charts, models and specimens and a carefully catalogued collection of these will help all the teachers to realize what is available in relation to any particular topic. She may also like to organize a central store of waste material, junk, paper and metal offcuts. The headteacher has greater authority and therefore greater persuasive powers when begging than class teachers often have, though all members of staff may have special opportunities through husbands and relations to obtain particular materials from factories or stores. If a list of books in the reference library can be collated with these resources, teachers will be stimulated to make intelligent use of materials and books. Small pamphlet-type reference books and free instruction manuals or catalogues can be stored in the resource department and card-indexed. In fact, the headteacher may assume or delegate responsibility for every kind of teacher resource material in her school, including radio, television, tape recorders, projectors and other visual aids which must be kept in working order. She will also probably wish to see that mechanical aids are used frequently and appropriately. Some heads also take responsibility for the school reference library, placing books of reference in a suitable storage space, properly labelled and classified, so that both children and teachers become familiar with the system and can fetch books as required, use and return them. The head has a special responsibility to maintain fairness in the sharing of rooms, facilities and equipment and by virtue of her position she alone can be the ultimate source of reference (though heads of large schools frequently delegate this responsibility, or it becomes part of the work of a teacher with a special responsibility allowance for language teaching throughout the school).

Many heads now think that the quality of work in the integrated day improves if the school relates consciously to the outside environment. If there is a college of education in the neighbourhood, the school will probably be used for teaching practice and the head, with her teachers, may be asked to consider together with the college how to make the best use of the students. Weak students can be a handicap, but reasonably competent students can provide a fund of new thinking and ideas, give help with particular groups of children who need special attention, bring in new skills and help in taking children on visits. Colleges are often anxious to put on courses for teachers or to make their library facilities available if approached by headteachers. The role of the college in the school, and the role of the students on teaching practice are important subjects for teachers' staff-meetings and college tutors will often be gratified if asked to take part in helping to define these roles. Such questions of general policy such as whether there should be a PTA and the form it should take, and whether or in what capacities parents should be invited into the school, are also important questions for the head to talk over with her teachers. The purpose, number and destination of visits to outside places of interest might also be discussed and decided, together with the kind of work that can result, though of course teachers will make their own suggestions for visits for their classes or groups. There is also the question of inviting outside speakers for the children's benefit or for the staff. Some schools have parents with special interests and knowledge who will, if the head and staff request it, come and talk or demonstrate to appropriate groups of children. There are also official bodies such as the police, fire service, road safety officials, librarians who are usually available on request. These contacts are mainly in the hands of the headteacher but might be requested by the staff. Some heads invite teachers who are doing particularly interesting work to visit their schools and explain their work to the staff during the time set apart for staff meetings. Advisory staff and college lecturers may be persuaded to find time to come into school to demonstrate various techniques, with or without children.

Organizing a room for the integrated day needs much planning, and takes time, and much of the work must be done on the spot in the classroom. Many headteachers try to organize free time for their staffs during the school week. Some heads take the school assembly themselves on certain days, leaving the teachers free to prepare their rooms. Some organize story sessions for two combined classes, in other cases classes may join together for community singing, or the head may take a class or group of children for a particular occupation. Since children in any one class may often be working on individual projects, but need to feel that they are working in cooperation with others, class-mixing when appropriate can be encouraged by the headteacher and this has the added advantage of lessening the demands on any one teacher. In the same way, it may be helpful to encourage some teacher specialization, perhaps in music or some aspects of the arts such as pottery or drama.

In conclusion amid all this thought on how to organize the school so that the integrated day runs smoothly and purposefully, headteachers particularly emphasized the need to remember that the school exists for the children and that it is the children who are of prime importance. In integrated day schools heads commonly structure the kind of integration that develops in line with the needs of the particular children in the particular school, while also trying to ensure that they continue to have a soundly based and wide ranging education, without any lowering of standards.

Many heads feel that they have a special responsibility towards three types of child: the able, the slow and the retiring. Heads say that they can ensure that the most able children are stretched to their full capacity by catering well for their exceptional abilities, by rapidly taking up and furthering their interests and by ensuring that all aspects of their education are covered, for example some able children would spend all day reading and writing without wishing to achieve or even notice anything creative. However, it is not only in verbal or mathematical fields that children may show particular gifts and some heads are better placed than their class teachers to notice children who show abilities in music or the arts and to provide for them.

Headteachers also seem to feel an equally special responsibility for ensuring that the slow learner is catered for, particularly by arranging much individual help and contact with adults. Perhaps the most difficult responsibility of all is the retiring child, who may be quiet, unaggressive, silent, making contact with only one or two close friends. In the words of one headmistress, 'such children can precipitate to a middle mediocrity', and this can perhaps happen more easily than ever with full vertical grouping or team teaching, and an integrated programme. One head keeps a special watch over these more difficult children both by her visits to the classroom and the group activities she stimulates outside. She throws her net wide by displays, collections and stories intended to get special responses, by appeals for help and by taking aside a group of children to continue their work further. Sometimes she may make a special time and place for reading a story or poetry, or listening to music and those who wish may come to share it. She and her teachers also make constant use of children's records.

Headteachers usually find the need to make themselves available to parents. There are many ways of achieving this, some of which have been dealt with in the first section of this chapter while others are discussed more fully in Chapter 8.

We may summarize the work of the headteacher in the words of the Plowden Committee in *Children and their Primary Schools*:

> It is for the headteacher in cooperation with the staff to crystallize the school's aims and to see that schemes and organizations serve them. The headteacher must know the staff, both the teachers and others, be aware of their gifts and their weaknesses, and assign their duties in such a way that the children are well taught. It is also the headteacher's responsibility to ensure that the staff are provided with essential equipment and are kept in touch with new ideas.
>
> It is rare to find a primary school so large that the headteacher cannot know every child . . . the best way to get to know children is to teach them and be with them inside and outside the classroom. In this way a good headteacher can stimulate the children, inspire the staff, weld the school into a unity and set its values. If there are areas of a curriculum which other teachers cannot effectively cover the headteacher will have to equip himself as far as possible to deal with them.

We found in our study of schools with an integrated day that headteachers commonly had these ideas in mind while giving them an individual interpretation.

Chapter 5

THE TEACHER IN THE INTEGRATED DAY

Having considered the organization of work areas and decided on a plan for the room, teachers have also to make an initial decision as to how the daily programme will be arranged. We found that in most schools there was a definite school policy which expressed itself in certain fixed points in the day, i.e. times of entering and leaving school, playtimes and school assembly. In some schools, all children entered school together at a fixed time, in others the teachers were expected to be in the building by 8.15 or 8.30 and the children came into the classroom or the home base individually, as they arrived at school. Some schools had playtime both morning and afternoon, some in the morning only while others, feeling that the integrated day with its free choices no longer imposed such a strain on the children, had done away with playtime altogether, leaving teachers to organize themselves in pairs for their coffee break so that one went for coffee while the other supervised two classes. School assemblies might be held at the beginning, end or middle of the morning, while some schools held two assemblies in the day, one in the morning and the other at the end of the afternoon. Some large schools organized two assemblies in the week for older children and two for younger, perhaps with the nursery classes, while the fifth morning would be an assembly for the whole school. These fixed points, however arranged, are the bones of the structure onto which the teacher arranges her interpretation of the integrated day, usually in consultation with her colleagues but still organizing her timetable individually.

The daily plans drawn up by three teachers are given below showing three variations on the theme of the integrated day within three differently structured schools.

Miss Tonkins's plan

Miss Tonkins is an experienced teacher working with a chronologically-grouped class of seven year olds in a large infant school which serves an educational priority area, but her plan might also suit an inexperienced teacher who wishes to begin working an integrated day. Miss Tonkins normally works a much freer system but this year her class presents special difficulties and she feels that the more closely controlled, though still integrated, day helps them by giving them an ordered framework which is conspicuously lacking in their home lives.

8.20	Arrives at school. Arranges the room, prepares materials, cuts paper, checks the clay, makes the paste, puts out cookery equipment.
8.50	Children come into classroom, register is marked and news exchanged.
9.00	School assembly.
9.30	Back in the classroom. Takes whole class for a talk about the day's programme. Children are divided into groups of about six according to their needs and interests noted the previous day. Each group is allotted two tasks in different areas with something extra in case a child finishes early. The groups change areas about 10.05 but any child who is still engaged on his first piece of work may still stay to finish it or carry it with him.
10.40	Playtime.
10.55	Each group moves to another work area with a new piece of work to undertake.
11.30	The whole class is called together for discussion, reading or viewing of interesting work done. Problems raised or solved are discussed. Sometimes word building is done in this time and throughout the half-hour particular attention is given to the development of language.
12.00	Home-time or school dinner.
1.30	Group work with two tasks for each group, the changeover coming at about 2.10.
2.45	Big clear-up of materials and room.
3.00	Playtime.
3.15	Story, poetry and/or music.
3.45	Home-time, most of the children having covered work in five different areas during the day but children who wished to stay at one lengthy piece of work having been able to do this.

Miss Tonkins remains in school until about 5.00 during which time she prepares for each group for the following day, planning work for those who need to move on, deciding who is in difficulties and needs her help, and checking that there is enough material for the children who need to continue practising what they were doing today. All these plans are written down in a page-a-day diary. Miss Tonkins also clears up the room and leaves it tidy. She goes home with a list of information and materials to be found for the following day.

Mrs Owen's plan

Mrs Owen is another experienced teacher working with a vertically-grouped class of five to six and a half year olds in an educationally advantaged area. The school has five classes and its own nursery.

8.30 Arrives at school. Meets colleagues in staffroom to exchange news and information about the day's programme.

8.45 In the classroom, gets out new material for a particular child or group of children. Sees that enough material is available for all, cuts paper, checks clay, makes paste, mixes paint as necessary. She expects the children to get out for themselves all material with which they are familiar.

8.55 Children come into school but go individually straight to assembly which is at 9.00.

9.20 In the classroom the whole class meets together. Mrs Owen hands out specific tasks to children who have special needs and directs certain other children to particular work areas. She shows the class the new materials that are available and demonstrates their use.

9.40 The children who have not been directed choose their work and get out their materials. They have been taught that, unless engaged on some lengthy piece of work like a needlework picture, they must each day do a piece of writing of some kind and spend some time on their mathematics which is organized on a structured syllabus. At this time the teacher always takes one group for some definite teaching.

10.40 About this time Mrs Owen goes for her coffee break. As there is no playtime for the children, the class is supervised as necessary by the teacher next door and in turn, Mrs Owen does the same for her.

10.55 On two days in the week, there is a TV programme for the whole class. On the other three days, Mrs Owen takes the youngest children for beginning work in reading or mathematics, or else helps them to work on their own project. The older children continue their own work.

11.55 All children go either to school dinner or home, leaving the room ready for continuing their work in the afternoon.

If the weather is wet and the room has to be used in the dinner hour, Mrs Owen just clears away the materials in the writing area and the library area.

1.30 Children return and continue their work.

2.45 A thorough clear-up now takes place.

3.00 Story and poetry. (Three days a week Mrs Owen takes music, recorders and percussion band with other classes. An NNEB student or the remedial teacher takes the story with Mrs Owen's class or they double-up with another class.)

3.30 Children go home.

Note

1 PE and movement are taken at fixed 'hall times' — the children just putting down their work and resuming it after the lesson.

2 Each child chooses when he will drink his milk so long as no more than four are sitting at the milk table.

From 3.30–5.00 Mrs Owen remains in school to prepare work for the next day. She plans the work for particular children and decides what new materials will be needed. Since, where possible, she teaches a new process to groups of children, who drop what they are doing when she calls them to form a group, and afterwards return to it, she needs to make a plan for the content and timing of these definite teaching periods, although she will also spontaneously call a group together if a teaching opportunity occurs. All her plans for the next day are written in her personal record book. In addition, she completes and checks her reading and mathematics record books and also reckons to spend about half an hour putting up work on the walls, making work books, mounting pictures etc. Mrs Owen makes work cards during the day, on the spot as needed, using slips of cardboard kept ready for the purpose so on the whole these are not part of her overnight preparation. Like Miss Tonkins she goes home with a list of information and materials to be obtained.

Mrs Jones's plan

Mrs Jones is a teacher of varied experience teaching in a six-class school which is organized for team-teaching in a very varied semirural area. Teachers are responsible for a specialist room (e.g. language and reading, mathematics, creative work etc, for a fortnight and then move on to another). Much of the teaching is organzied for small groups through programmed learning from tape recorders with headphones. In these circumstances, Miss Jones's plan is really part of the general plan formulated together by all the teachers.

8.40 Meets colleagues in staffroom to exchange information about the day's programme.

8.50 Each teacher meets her children in the home base and registers are taken.

9.00 All staff and children meet for discussion of the day's work. Each teacher explains anything new that will be available in the room for which she is responsible. The groups that have been arranged for definite teaching are told the time and the room for their lesson. Each child then decides in which room he will start the day's work, though free choice is limited by the number of children who can be accommodated at one time, so some children may have to start with their second choice and move later to their real preference. The pattern of the morning then follows Mrs Owen's plan except that there is a definite clearing up and tidying period at the end of the morning. The children are trained to put a tick on a record chart when they have done a piece of work in reading, mathematics and art/craft. The teachers check these records in the dinner break.

1.30 Meeting with all teachers and children. Those children whose records were not found satisfactory are reminded to finish covering their three areas of work. Groups are told when and where they will specifically work with the teacher. The children then move to the various rooms and work until about 2.45 when there is a period of thorough clearing-up and tidying.

3.00 Often a story is told, sometimes to all the children together but sometimes they return to their home bases for a story from their own teachers. Sometimes they may have a choice between story, music or drama organized in three separate rooms.

3.30 Home-time for the children. The teachers stay on for a conference during which the work is discussed and plans are made for the following day. Mrs Jones has then to check the work record of the children in her own class and prepare her room for the following day so that children who need to progress to new work have the necessary work cards and equipment or the tape recorder is adequately programmed for them. Like all the other teachers, Mrs Jones then writes up a record of the work done in her room during the day so that when she hands over to another teacher at the end of a fortnight, it is clear what has been taught and the direction in which work is moving.

These three plans have been drawn up to suit schools which serve different social areas and are organized in different ways. But within the same school, each teacher tends to build up her own individual interpretation of the integrated day. To illustrate this point, we include here two accounts written by young teachers in their second and third years of teaching who are working in the same school. The official school day is structured on the following pattern:

Children enter school individually as soon as they arrive.

9.00–10.15	Children's work.
10.15–10.30	Playtime.
10.30–11.00	School assembly.
11.00–12.00	Children's work.
12.00	Home-time or school dinner.
1.15–2.20	Children's work.
2.20–2.35	Playtime.
2.35–3.05	Story, music, drama, poetry, etc.
3.05–3.15	School assembly and home-time.
3.15–4.15	Teachers prepare work in the school for the next day.

The individual plans are as follows:

My integrated day (D. Smith)

I arrive at school at 8.40 and begin to prepare the room for the daily activities. The school day is divided into three periods. I divide the class into three groups of mixed ability. There are four main topics to cover in a day, written work, mathematics, reading, creative work and three main periods in which to do it, so I include reading and creative work in the same period since the reading needs individual attention while the group needs far less help with its creative work.

At each period in the school day one of my groups is doing some form of written work (news, story, sounds or comprehension), one of the groups is doing mathematics (measuring, weighing, time and pure number), while the third group is spending some time reading individually and doing creative work — painting, clay, collage, models, or playing in the Wendy House, with musical instruments or sand. I also hear as many of this group as possible read aloud. For me this has worked well with a class of forty. I know by the end of the day that each child has done some written and mathematical work, read to himself or to me and had an opportunity to do some form of creative work or play in the sand or Wendy House.

I record when they have done their work by ticking a list I carry around with me so by the end of the day I should have two ticks by each name, one for mathematics and one for writing.

No period is rigidly defined and if a child wants to spend more time on a particular piece of work he continues in the next period.

My integrated day (G. Williams)

Arrival at school is at 8.30 and part of the room is prepared for creative activities.

As the children arrive they all have their own particular job for each week, worked on a rota system and they prepare the classroom for the day, i.e. chairs are arranged, creative materials other than those I have supplied are got out, library books are checked, junk boxes are tidied, paint and paper are supplied etc.

The first ten to fifteen minutes are taken up with registration and discussion of the day's programme, usually of the first period, as well as discussing news or any particular topics that have arisen. The twenty-six children then split into three groups, and do alternately number work, creative activity or writing. The writing activity includes their news or a story as well as a writing pattern, and I will generally hear all the group read individually except when it is the youngest group and we have a short period of flash card work and reading from a wall story. There are three major periods of work a day interspersed with PE, music and movement, music and nature study and broadcasts and thus the children may move from one subject to another over the periods. Each period is started with a short discussion of the work to be completed. The younger children, when they have finished, may choose from a selection of reading and number toys while the older children use number games or reading and sound games.

The major drawback of the integrated day is the supervision of each group. Obviously I am available for help all the time, but when helping an older group with reading and writing or a younger group with flash cards then there is less supervision of creative work and vice versa and I must arrange work that the children can cope with while unsupervised for a short time.

Maths such as graphs, measuring and time are generally done as a class activity and that day the children will generally miss some time of a working period that should be, say, devoted to creative work. This must be amended the next day by allowing more freedom in what the child chooses to do when he has finished his work.

Each child's progress is ticked off in a record book which I mark while the work is going on, for I find this the easiest method of checking that every child has completed a certain amount of work each day.

The working day ends at afternoon playtime with five to ten minutes of clearing up with the allocated jobs being performed again. This is also the library time when each child may choose a book to take home, but he must write its title on his card, or the librarian for that week must do it, and also check it off when the book is returned.

The last period is devoted to story, drama, music or poetry and is usually a quiet peaceful class activity which brings the class together to round off the day.

All teachers in this school have three main work periods to arrange. The most obvious difference between the plans developed by Miss Williams and Miss Smith lies in the way they allocate the learning of basic skills within these periods. Miss Williams divides the field of study into three sections: 1 language study; 2 mathematics; 3 creative arts, whereas Miss Smith divides the work into four parts: 1 hand-writing, recording and composition; 2 mathematics; 3 reading; 4 creative arts and then she works reading and creative work together for one group in each period. Both young teachers seem happy with their own form of organization which both suits their individual views of the children's needs and fits into the main school pattern.

We found that most teachers, even the very experienced, found it necessary to write down the plans they made for the next day's work. These plans were kept in various forms — page-a-day diaries, record books, loose sheets of paper pinned to a board in the classroom, postcards kept for reference in the teacher's pocket and later filed. Teachers were usually willing to let us see their plans, examples of which are given below.

Entry from daily record

Projects

1 Apollo 16 — find cylinders, cut card for cones.
John, Ben — write labels for their picture in group book.
Jonathan — write about walking on moon.

2 Hey diddle diddle picture — make papier mâché for spoon and plate.

3 Roads — send Braden and Alan to find book on old roads.
Make long thin books for pictures and writing.
Remind Paul to finish model of bulldozer.

Maths

Blue group	Record 123 pattern on 100 sq. (Karen to finish Unifix pattern).
Red group	Continue measuring.
Green group	Six collections in sets.
Yellow group	Cuisenaire patterns for pink.
Purple group	Cuisenaire free play (space rocket?).

Reading, writing and word work

Group B	learn 'or'
Group E	practise c, a, g.

Music

Recorders group 1, add G.
Remind NNEB student to encourage Andrew and Nicole to draw and paint etc and to talk of what they are doing.
Feed the tadpoles — who will?

Daily programme
My class is divided into five groups, six children in each.

1st	red group	writing area
2nd	blue group	mathematics area
3rd	grey group	art and craft area
4th	yellow group	reading area
5th	green group	centre of room and practical area

Entry from page-a-day diary, April 24th

Red group
Using dictionaries. Writing connected with story of Robin Hood and his Merry Men. Whom he met, what did he do? Make picture story book.

Blue group
Working from number books *Starting Number* p. 4 counting on and back, (or carrying on from where you left off).

Grey group
Frieze of Sherwood Forest. Using wallpaper, coloured paper etc. *Then* Robin Hood and his Merry Men. Using material, wallpaper, bits of waste material from junk box. Draw shape first.

Yellow group
Reading books and phonic box with initial sounds to be done while waiting to read.

Green group
Lotto game with words that need extra practice from reading books.
Word-building box with individual letters, making words children unsure of, e.g. Dean must try to do his second name.
Pairs game 'how, why and where'.

When the plans for the day have been made, the teachers have the task of implementing the plan and teaching the children or causing them to learn. There is no doubt that the integrated day makes greater demands on the teachers than any other form of teaching but teachers also seem to find it the most rewarding. As one teacher said, 'Integration is not just a matter of planning and assigning tasks, "You do number, you writing, you handwork", but of choosing interests and getting the most out of them in as many aspects as possible, exploiting situations, seeing their possibilities. For instance, we are keeping chickens and we have come up against the cost of food, the increase in weight of the chicks and the fact that they do not all grow at the same rate, and how they eat more as they get older.'

In developing interests, most teachers seem to find some form of record helps them to keep in mind exactly what is happening, what has been suggested, and the general direction of the work as it grows. There are many ways of keeping records of centres of interest. Some teachers write up daily or weekly a straightforward record of what has happened, together with the part played by individual children. But the most popular form of record (because it is quickly made and easy to refer to), seems to be the flow chart, which records diagrammatically how one aspect of an interest flows and develops into another. Sometimes the chart will show a straightforward flow, if all the group is united in working together. An example of this is the flow chart (p. 104) of an interest in spring flowers by a group of six year old girls.

In developing this interest, all five girls worked together throughout and the flow chart records simply the development of one interest into another. However, some interests may begin as class interests from which individual children or groups choose different aspects for more detailed study. The flow chart then assumes a different pattern. Instead of one stream flowing along, the original interest becomes like a central lake from which many streams flow out. An example of this is the flow chart of an interest in fire engines developed by a vertically-grouped class (see p. 105).

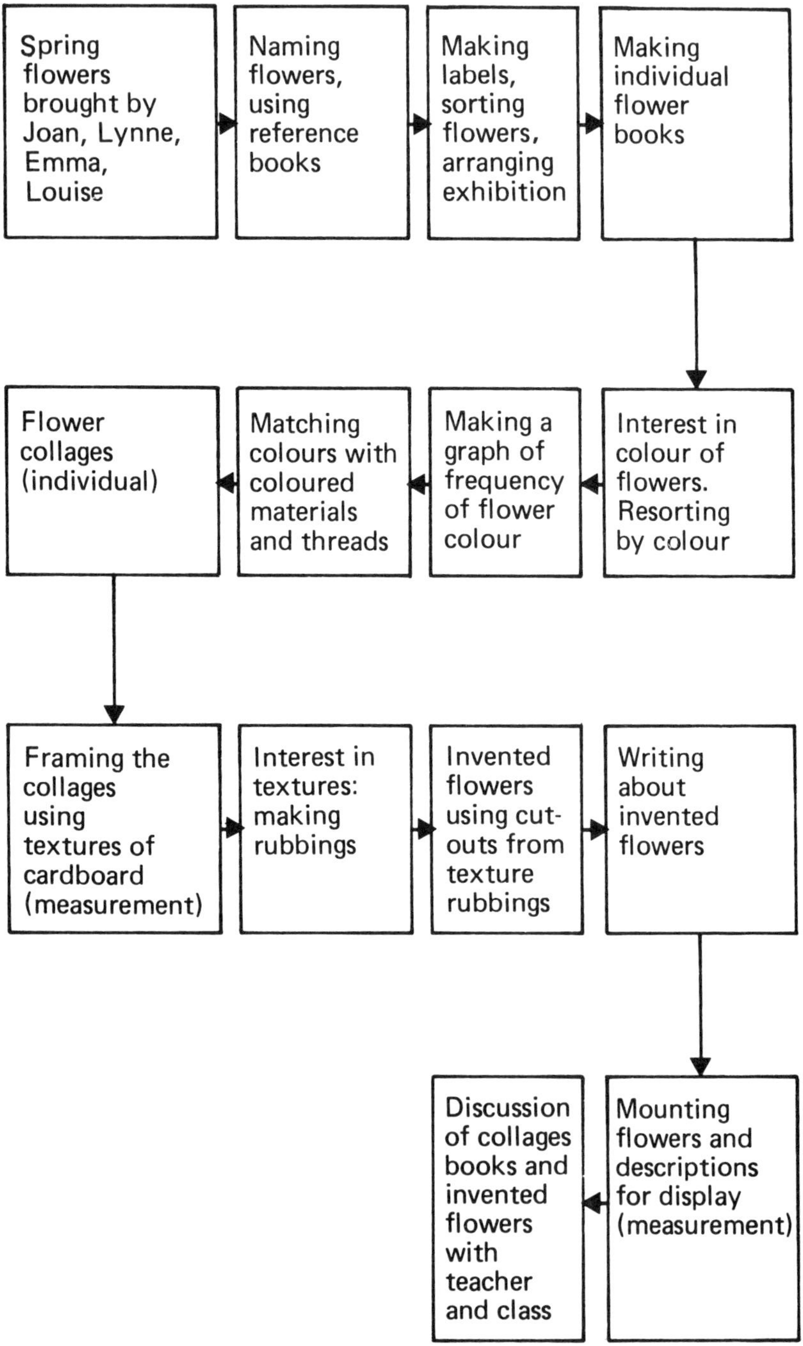
Spring flowers brought by Joan, Lynne, Emma, Louise
Naming flowers, using reference books
Making labels, sorting flowers, arranging exhibition
Making individual flower books
Interest in colour of flowers. Resorting by colour
Making a graph of frequency of flower colour
Matching colours with coloured materials and threads
Flower collages (individual)
Framing the collages using textures of cardboard (measurement)
Interest in textures: making rubbings
Invented flowers using cut-outs from texture rubbings
Writing about invented flowers
Mounting flowers and descriptions for display (measurement)
Discussion of collages books and invented flowers with teacher and class

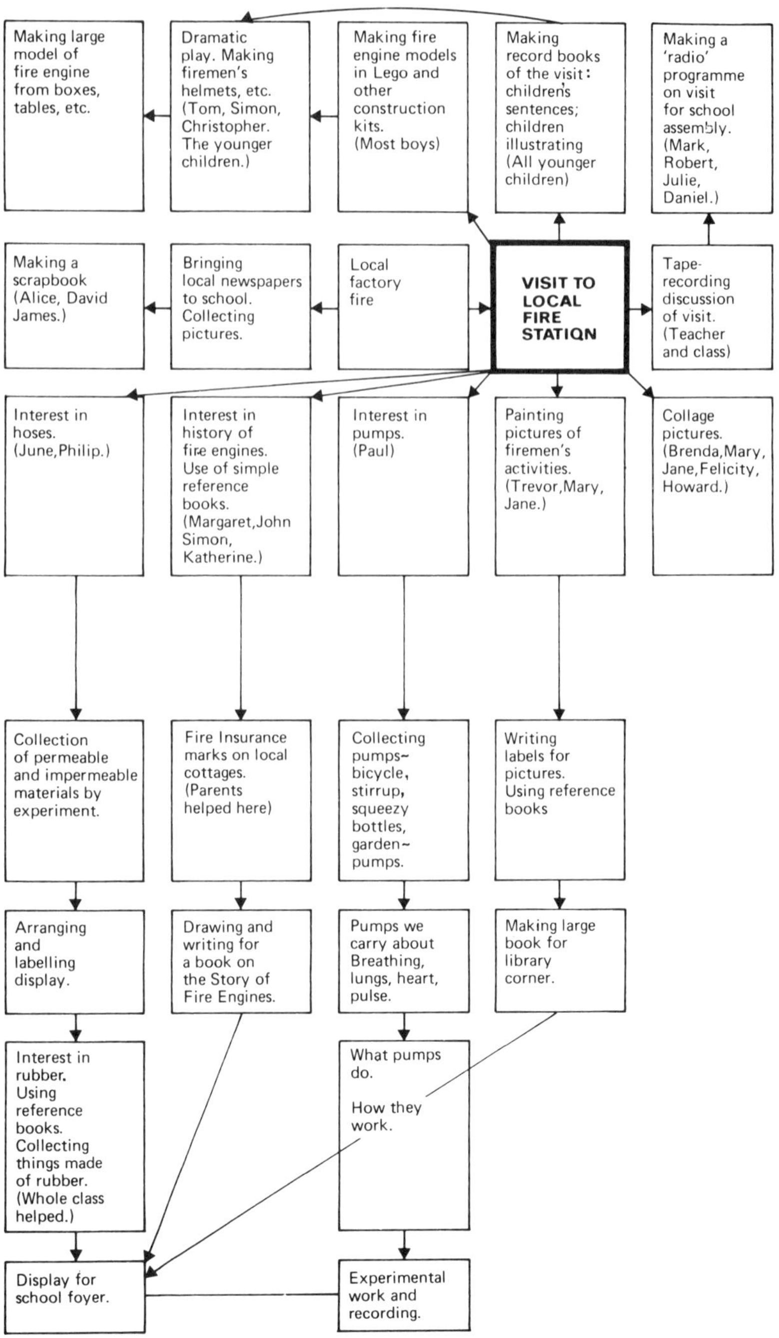
Making large model of fire engine from boxes, tables, etc.
Dramatic play. Making firemen's helmets, etc. (Tom, Simon, Christopher. The younger children.)
Making fire engine models in Lego and other construction kits. (Most boys)
Making record books of the visit: children's sentences; children illustrating (All younger children)
Making a 'radio' programme on visit for school assembly. (Mark, Robert, Julie, Daniel.)
Making a scrapbook (Alice, David James.)
Bringing local newspapers to school. Collecting pictures.
Local factory fire
VISIT TO LOCAL FIRE STATION
Tape-recording discussion of visit. (Teacher and class)
Interest in hoses. (June, Philip.)
Interest in history of fire engines. Use of simple reference books. (Margaret, John Simon, Katherine.)
Interest in pumps. (Paul)
Painting pictures of firemen's activities. (Trevor, Mary, Jane.)
Collage pictures. (Brenda, Mary, Jane, Felicity, Howard.)
Collection of permeable and impermeable materials by experiment.
Fire Insurance marks on local cottages. (Parents helped here)
Collecting pumps~ bicycle, stirrup, squeezy bottles, garden~ pumps.
Writing labels for pictures. Using reference books
Arranging and labelling display.
Drawing and writing for a book on the Story of Fire Engines.
Pumps we carry about Breathing, lungs, heart, pulse.
Making large book for library corner.
Interest in rubber. Using reference books. Collecting things made of rubber. (Whole class helped.)
What pumps do.
How they work.
Display for school foyer.
Experimental work and recording.

From this diagram the following points emerge very clearly:

1 The interest of the younger children is less wide-ranging and of shorter duration than the interests of the older children so that they have exhausted the possibilities while the older children are still happily working along. Obviously stimulus for a new interest will be needed by this group.
2 Three children show scientific interests aroused by pumps and hoses, and are able to work on them individually for a long time.
3 Some groups have done creative work throughout while others have used a greater variety of skills — reading, writing, drawing, constructional work. In planning future centres of interest, the teacher can see which children need to balance up their work.
4 Some subjects have had no place in this centre of interest, i.e. mathematics, music, PE and need separate provision.

Teachers often find that compiling such a flow chart makes the complicated pattern of class behaviour and learning clearer than a purely verbal statement.

In fact, most teachers of young children find that they must have a very wide range of knowledge even to see the possibilities of the children's interests and questions. They are expected to understand the structure of language and to be able to use it accurately and flexibly. The knowledge and critical evaluation of various methods of teaching reading is supposed to be part of their professional equipment. They need to have a sufficiently wide knowledge of mathematics to appreciate all the possibilities of the material they present to the children. In addition, they must have scientific, musical, artistic and physical skills if some of the children in their class are not to be educationally deprived. How much is demanded from the teacher in the integrated day, and how seriously many teachers take the possibilities of their work, is illustrated by the objectives of their teaching of art, craft and science, as stated by two teachers, together with the implication of what they have said which we have added in brackets.

Objectives of arts and crafts in the integrated day

1 They develop manual dexterity. (The teacher needs to be able to handle skilfully a variety of tools.)

2 They cater for the world of reality and the world of fantasy, both of which are necessary to the development of the personality. (The teacher needs an awareness of things and a developed imagination.)

3 Arts and crafts have a definite therapeutic function in providing a legitimate outlet for self-expression and the release of tension and frustration. (The teacher can learn much from the observation of a child's attitude to his creative work and needs to be a skilled observer.)

4 In encouraging artistic interests in the young child, a foundation may be laid for an interest in creative hobbies in later life. Some children discover very early a natural aptitude. (The teacher must possess a variety of skills.)

5 Seeking to make images from the world around, the child develops a more critical awareness and perception will be heightened. (The teacher needs awareness, sensitivity and perception.)

6 Later the child will develop a more discriminating ability and begin to distinguish the worthwhile from the mediocre.

(The teacher needs developed powers of discrimination and taste.)

Objectives of science in the integrated day

1 Primarily to promote an atmosphere of pleasure and interest in science which will stimulate the children's curiosity about natural phenomena. (The teacher must be intelligently curious.)

2 To provide materials which the children can explore and evaluate at their own level of ability. (The teacher needs to be aware of the techniques of scientific exploration and the language of evaluation.)

3 To encourage individual thinking and judgment, and to develop techniques of accurate observation, reasoning and the ability to solve problems. (The teacher must be capable of scientific thinking.)

4 To help children to appreciate the need to treat some things differently from others and to be aware of, and to provide, the necessities for supporting life and realize the need for conservation. (The teacher must have some awareness of the interdependence of life forms and an understanding of environmental issues.)

5 To engage in the classification of materials. (The teacher needs to understand the principles of classification and a variety of standard methods of recording classifications.)

It can be seen from these teachers' statements of their objectives in what are only two facets of their teaching, that they see themselves as obliged to think out the long-term implications of the activities they present to children and aware of the diversity of knowledge and skills required in working with young children. This awareness was shared by most of the integrated day teachers that we met. In fact, one experienced teacher remarked, 'I didn't really start to become educated until I started the integrated day. Then I found that I had so much to learn to satisfy the children.' The Plowden Committee in *Children and their Primary Schools* expressed this aspect of the teacher's work very clearly:

> As we have surveyed the way children learn, the demands made on teachers have appeared frighteningly high. The primary school curriculum must touch on the scientific and mathematical knowledge on which the modern world

depends and in which children are particularly interested. The teacher who used to give set lessons could manage on a little knowledge and use it over and over again. Far more knowledge, both about subject matter and about how children learn, is called for in teachers who have continually to exercise judgment, to 'think on their feet', to keep in mind long-term and short-term objectives. They have to select an environment which will encourage curiosity, to focus attention on enquiries which will lead to useful discovery, to collaborate with children, to lead from behind.

We found that teachers working the integrated day stressed time and time again their need to equip themselves more fully for the task and indicated the various ways in which they achieved this. Many said that within their schools teachers now have more freedom in school time to exchange and discover new ideas and to use the facilities available, such as the staff library, the radio and television programmes. Advice and information given by head-teachers, advisory staffs and local inspectors was another factor and particularly appreciated by inexperienced teachers. More and more teachers want to attend courses, visit other schools, teachers centres and workshops, to listen to radio and television programmes on various aspects of their work, to read and use professional libraries, and then to discuss, experiment and discuss again.

Teachers themselves seemed to see their role in the integrated day as exacting but stimulating and rewarding. In the main it was described as developing social awareness and stimulating intellectual development. In a group of young children it is frequently the teacher who must initiate and maintain social contact and always the teacher who sets the standards of sympathy, kindness and courtesy with which these contacts are made. Many teachers explicitly stated ways in which they used opportunities created by the freer integrated situation such as helping children to take turns or to understand the point of view of another child, for example 'But Carol and Ben are using that book just now so will you do this until they have finished?' 'But John wants it as much as you do', 'She wants to be quiet so you do that over here, will you?' Teachers saw in an integrated day a situation which helped them to build a child's sense of identity by enabling them to discover what a slow child can do rather than what he cannot, and thus develop his concept of himself as an achiever.

Teachers saw part of their social role in the integrated day as providing an audience before which developing skills could be displayed and approved. Sometimes the teacher herself was the audience, 'Come and look at this, Miss Smith,' or sometimes she stimulated the other children to form an audience, 'Who would like to look at the play that Hilary's friends have made?' When the teacher sat with a group of children to listen to a performance she was teaching the children how to be an audience. Teachers saw themselves as having increased opportunities for rendering physical care, protection and comfort to children where it was required, and then showing children in their turn how they could render these services to other children and, on occasion, to herself. Children in a vertically-grouped class have particular opportunities for catching this attitude of service if the teacher displays it, for there are always some older children who are good at comforting, helping with work difficulties, tying bows and knots, tidying, finding mislaid articles, remembering messages, taking younger children round the building, buttoning coats. And as one teacher remarked, 'There is all the difference in the world between just buttoning a child into a coat and doing it as though you loved it.'

Teachers also saw the integrated day as enabling them more easily to provide a setting of happiness and pleasure for the children. They were more able to chat informally with children or groups and get their point of view. They were able to play with children who desired social contact with an adult or whose ideas of play were limited. There were many opportunities for laughter and jokes which not only made the atmosphere light and gay but also gave groups a feeling of social cohesion or 'togetherness'.

Where the intellectual development of children is concerned, teachers saw the demands of the integrated day as changing their role from the giver of accepted wisdom to the stimulator of ideas and the provider of ways and means. Where necessary the teachers were ready to contribute information but they were more occupied in showing children how to obtain information for themselves, by teaching them how to find and use relevant books, pointing out appropriate TV or radio programmes, stimulating them to ask people questions and often simply taking them to look and feel and hear on the spot. In most schools working an integrated day we found children engaged in organized exploration of some facet of the school building, or grounds, or out with some adult on a visit (see Chapter 8), to gather information or material.

There was much discussion as to whether teachers should see

themselves mainly as stimulators of children's ideas, helping them to develop what has occurred spontaneously from the material provided. Some teachers, however, were convinced that they needed to go to school each day with ideas of their own, even where the children had been working spontaneously and with enthusiasm the day before, in case 'they've gone off it' — a phrase which every teacher of young children will understand. When this happened it was felt that the teacher could only help with a new idea or direction of investigation, which should always be ready in the teacher's mind, in the hope that they will later 'come back to it'.

As providers for children in the integrated day, teachers have an absorbing task in ensuring that each work area has enough materials and a programme of activities sufficiently full and varied to hold the attention of each child using that area. Even in a chronologically-grouped class, work and materials to suit a wide range of abilities will be needed to challenge both a slow learning child and an advanced child. With a vertically-grouped class a very wide range of material will be needed indeed. Successful activities tend to be activities that have been planned as far ahead as needed, with work themes decided upon by the children, or the teacher and children together, and then the appropriate apparatus and equipment assembled. Many teachers recommend that a clear plan be made of the week's work and that this should then be broken down into a work plan for each day, bearing in mind that the children may well 'go off it', or that a group may suddenly perceive a new and fruitful line of investigation. There is often a dilemma for teachers here as to how far children need to be helped to keep to the point and where they should be encouraged to follow a new lead.

An example of this was shown by a group of seven year old boys, making furniture for a Wendy House involving accurate measuring, who produced a grandfather clock with two pendulums. 'Do clocks have two pendulums?' asked the teacher. Investigation established the fact but the boys had become fascinated by the mechanics of the pendulum — 'How far? For how long? Longer or shorter string? What for?' And the teacher asked, 'What pattern does the swing make?' So that the teacher's problem now became, 'Do we work on the pendulum and hope to return to the furniture? Or do we complete the furniture and hope to return to the pendulum?'

In providing work for all levels of ability, work cards are widely used by most integrated day teachers, even where children can read very little, since a few key words such as count, draw, sort, weigh etc followed by pictures or put in a box with appropriate material can provide a wealth of stimulus for using material. There are two main types of work cards:

1 Cards designed to stimulate children to explore the possibilities of materials, e.g.
  This book is about ships. What are their names? Draw them. Show them to the class. You could make a model ship. Make a long thin man and a short fat man from boxes. Which can hold the most food?
2 Cards designed to provide practice in skills, e.g. writing cards, composition cards and cards for practising mathematical processes.

Experienced teachers usually provide both kinds of work cards for each work area though some, like Mrs Owen, write work cards for individual children or particular situations on the spot, but these are usually practice cards rather than those designed to initiate activities.

All integrated day teachers felt that they had greater opportunities of developing the children's language skills than under any other form of teaching. The daily discussion periods, the more informal organization and the frequent contact with adults other than the teacher herself mean that the children are provided with greatly increased language opportunities of which progressive teachers are willing to take the fullest advantage. Apart from talking with the children socially, teachers spend much time showing materials to children, explaining their origin, uses, similarities and differences in comparison with other materials, and in this process new words, phrases and sentence structures are learned. Examples of this important, informal language teaching are so frequent in the teacher's life that she may become almost automatic in simple language teaching, but actually a periodic analysis of her procedure may be revealing. For instance about words, 'What colour is it? Purple? Mauve? Lilac? Do you know, they are all different names for the same colour?' And teaching sentence structure, 'Don't just push it at me John, say "Please look at my picture".' And correcting sentence structure, the child asks the teacher to write, 'They was going market', but the teacher actually writes and the child reads, 'They were going to the market'. In discussion the children learn that different families call their main room the lounge, the drawing-room, the sitting-room, the front room, and that these are alternative names for the same room.

Language being a tool to describe, classify and explain our world, the adult by using language teaches children to 'decode' the world and is also able to grasp their misconceptions, for example a boy thought that a cricket bat was made of iron because it was hard and could hit a hard ball. The teacher was thus able to see his misconception and to show, both practically and verbally, other properties of iron so that he was able to make a more accurate 'decoding' of his data. Further, language enables children to begin to move away from thinking in the concrete terms of immediate experience towards the manipulation and comparison of experiences through words. For example, the boy who said, 'My father said that 25 is a quarter of 100 and I've been thinking, if 25 is the quarter of 100 then $12\frac{1}{2}$ is the eighth of a hundred', is manipulating experience verbally to produce a new fact which can be checked against further experience. And having painted striped patterns, a comparison by the whole group of individual results produced many verbal ideas as to how the designs could be combined to make more interesting results. The integrated day provides many opportunities for this 'iffing' or making hypotheses. Many teachers encourage children always to put forward a hypothesis before undertaking a piece of work, for example in cookery, 'What will happen if you have too much water? If the fat is left in lumps? If the fat is dropped on the floor?' and in mathematics, 'If we put two more cubes on this side and two more on that side, will it still balance?', for it is the ability to make verbal hypotheses which is a main factor in discovery. Teachers who analyse their own use of language and language teaching from time to time have found that the integrated day gives them great opportunities for all these various forms of language usage.

In the integrated day one of the most important roles the teacher plays is that of questioner who provoke responses and ideas. Inexperienced teachers often find this questioning role very difficult, for stimulating questioning requires knowledge and foresight about the type of answer required. In the beginning one asks or writes such questions as, 'Will you write a story for me?', 'Can you tie a bow?' or 'Have you done your weighing yet?' to which the answer is properly merely 'Yes' or 'No', whereas the experienced teacher will ask, 'What story can you write for us?', 'How much weighing have you done?' and write at the head of a chart, 'Tie bows. Write your name here', all of which require real linguistic responses. The question to provoke further ideas also needs experience. For example, a boy with an aunt in Canada, on receiving a packet of fifty Red Indian photographs, showed them to his inexperienced teacher who said, 'How nice, thank you for bringing them. Children, look at the photographs Robert has brought.' The class looked, and talked and Robert took his photographs home and nothing further happened. But next term he took them to an experienced teacher who asked, 'Where does your aunt live? On the map? What is it like? Does she see Indians? Yes? Which tribe?' etc and a whole term's work developed.

Even in the integrated day, children need to feel the security of a teacher who knows what she expects from them and has planned her work accordingly. In general, teachers felt that successful planning depended on three factors:

1 Thought about the ultimate objectives of teaching each subject or providing each activity, in order that the planning may serve these objectives and be continually referred back to them. For example, the objectives for art and craft, and for science given earlier in this chapter had been thoroughly discussed with colleagues and coloured the entire provision for these subjects in the school.
2 Consideration of the teacher's aim for each individual child in the class, partly on a long-term and partly on a day to day basis; for example a basic music lesson to play a tambourine in time to four beats in a bar, with the long term objective of teaching the child to play as a member of a band, and to give him a real feeling for music.
3 Knowledge of the standard of each particular class related to a basic standard of what might be achieved by children of each specific age. In most schools the head supplied a basic scheme of what might be expected in that school, in each particular subject or activity. Teachers particularly commended these basic schemes because they provided a framework within which all could see their respective parts and fit into the whole.

In a newly integrated situation there are two groups of teachers who may have special problems — the young probationary teachers and the experienced teachers who have taught for many years in more formal schools.

The young teacher

We have found that young teachers benefit greatly if they are able to visit their new school before taking up the appointment. This gives them the opportunity to see the children, make contact with colleagues and see the kind of integrated day system by which the school works and for which they must plan even before the first day of term. They can also glimpse the kind of social environment from which their children come and in relation to which they will teach. It has been found most helpful if basic school rules and work schedules are also explained during these preliminary visits, i.e. letter formation, reading scheme, number syllabus and rules about PE clothing and shoes, dinner-hour activities etc.

Many heads seem to give much thought to the size of class that a probationer teacher is given and to the situation of that class in the building, so that the probationer is not isolated but is rather placed next to an understanding and helpful experienced teacher who is willing to listen to the ideas of the newcomer and, if necessary, help her to translate them into satisfactory practice. We have found it particularly advantageous when there is an experienced teacher on the staff to whom the probationary teacher can turn at any time for help and encouragement as of right, in addition to the headmistress who is not always available. Sometimes this was an informal arrangement but sometimes a post of special responsibility had been given to a teacher who, in a large school, would be responsible for all teachers in the first two years of their service. In other large schools the deputy-head as well as the headmistress was free of responsibility for a class and her responsibilities included the professional welfare of the probationer teachers. It was felt in some schools that if the reorganization of teacher-training becomes effective, beginner-teachers might well be part of the responsibilities of the teacher who is designated student-tutor.

However, most teachers, whether inexperienced or not, felt that the more open aspects of the integrated day gave them increased opportunities for informal contacts and advice-seeking throughout the day. Young teachers could mention difficulties as they occurred and ask advice in the actual situation instead of waiting until afterwards. Older colleagues, with experience of particular difficulties, are able to discuss or explain on request in the living situation, and to offer quiet, tactful praise and unobtrusive hints as opportunities arise. Probationary teachers often find difficulty in displaying work to the best advantage but the integrated day where the work spills over into corridors, work areas and assembly halls means that all teachers have the opportunity of seeing one another's wall-charts, children's books, illustrations and displays which helps to disseminate ideas and raise the general standard.

One of the topics most frequently raised by young teachers when discussing the integrated day is the question of discipline. It is often felt that the freer day will lead to noisy, uncontrolled children and provide far too many opportunities for time-wasting or shirking work not immediately interesting. In general we have not found that the integrated day need result in increased noise. On the contrary, the quietness of the integrated, open-plan schools has been very striking and in North Hill School it was almost incredible that one hundred and sixty children were working freely in this open space. On the other hand, while no known organization of teaching has ever stopped all children from evading tasks or wasting their time if they were sufficiently determined, the integrated day does provide extra opportunities for time-wasters unless the teachers are particularly aware of the problem. Experienced teachers offered the following suggestions to help the young teacher see that each child as far as possible had a profitable day.

1 Careful attention to organization has been found a very important factor in securing maximum effort and attention. If the classroom is organized, with material and apparatus prepared before the children are ready to begin work, they start off in a purposeful atmosphere with challenges suitable to each child's level of development. Some teachers recommend that each day at least six things should be provided for children to choose from when they have finished planned occupations.
2 It has also been found conducive to maximum effort when the teacher has a clear understanding of the steps to be followed in developing children's knowledge and skills in each subject and plans her work so that the children themselves feel that they are progressing in power and control, and moving from one stage to another.
3 Children are made more secure by a structure of simple classroom rules, worked out by the teacher, to suit herself and

her children, within the framework of the general school order. Once these rules are made, they should be good-humouredly, but firmly, enforced or the children lose confidence in the teacher. This consistent firmness is often difficult for inexperienced teachers who sometimes hope that if they turn a blind eye, the inappropriate behaviour will go away. Three particularly important rules suggested by experienced teachers are:

1 All work begun should be completed. If a child starts a job he must finish it before moving on to another though the teacher may need in some cases to give a lot of help before the child can feel the satisfaction of a piece of work completed.
2 All work areas must be left tidy. Training in tidiness seems absolutely essential; children need to be taught to put materials away neatly whenever an individual job is finished, and to help in collective tidying of the classroom at stated times of the day.
3 No child may interfere with another child's work. There should be no interference with the work of children who leave the class for group work, e.g. recorder groups, reading groups, etc, or with work which is put on display or left out to dry.

4 The teacher's own manner has a great effect on the control and self-discipline of the children. It seems important that the teacher should be polite to the children, without condescension or 'talking down', and also expect politeness and good behaviour from the children. An attitude of kindly surprise when a child misbehaves, 'It isn't like you, John, why did you?' is often very effective, especially when coupled with praise and pleasure in efforts towards satisfactory work and mannerly behaviour. In fact, praise seems to be the main weapon of the experienced teachers in stimulating effort or good behaviour. (It is also suggested that teachers should expect or teach the conventional answers to questions such as 'How are you?', 'Are you better?', 'How old are you?', 'Where do you live?' and that, as children progress through the school, verbal answers to all questions should be required, not nods, grunts or gestures, even if the answer is 'I don't know'.)

5 Clear, positive directions are an aid to discipline. The directon 'Everyone pack away now' frequently leads to trouble, but if

with more foresight the teacher states, 'Time to pack away. Put your work away tidily. When you have finished, come and sit on the mats by me', the children know exactly what to do and are helped to finish in a controlled way. Positive suggestions also help. To the rather uncontrolled boy who said, 'I don't think I want to do any more of this', an experienced teacher replied, 'But you would like to finish it to help the others, I am sure.' 'Yes,' said the boy and did so.

6 Promoting an attitude of mutual cooperation helps to establish a climate in which self-control flourishes. An experienced teacher tends not only to suggest that the children help her but finds all kinds of ways in which they can help each other as well, such as knotting ties or fastening back buttons after PE, spelling words, accompanying a new or shy child, assisting in a long job or a very messy clearing-up, etc.

Finally, experienced teachers nearly all seem to remember their early struggles as probationer teachers and from these experiences to offer a kindly piece of advice to the young teacher. 'Most teachers will spend many years in the profession and the probationer cannot be expected to approach her best in the first few years. We all make mistakes. The important point is how much one learns from one's mistakes.'

The very experienced teacher

At the time when most very experienced teachers entered the profession, the usual organization was class teaching of chronologically-grouped classes and the standard of work was mainly concerned with attainment in the three RS so that children could pass 'the Scholarship' or the 11+ exam. Although they may have modernized their approach, this earlier experience has usually left mature teachers with what is almost a deep-rooted instinct about teaching, which is at variance with today's aim of responsibility for one's own education and the need to educate in a wider sense for a rapidly changing world.

We found that many mature teachers, wishing to change to the freer integrated day, hesitated to do so because a feeling of personal inadequacy and a sense that their teacher's 'instinct' would inhibit their ability to cope with freedom. However, where these very experienced teachers had agreed to 'have a go', the general finding is that they are very good at it and become some of the cream of the integrated day teachers. In the first place they usually have a deep understanding both of the children and the nature of the job. They are professionals in the deepest sense of the term. They also have 'got the language of it', a term which experienced teachers will understand, meaning that they know how to talk to children, how to put points across and enlist cooperation, how to organize and develop subject matter. Their standards, both of work and behaviour, are high and they are aware of what to expect and how to get it. So once a mature teacher has accepted the philosophy of the integrated day, she may well make the other teachers envious of her organizational and teaching ability, for formal teachers learned how to teach. Many experienced teachers, especially those in small village schools, find that they have been running an integrated day for years, without knowing it or ever using the term. Those who have made a change from really formal teaching usually say that they find the integrated day very stimulating and one mature teacher in her mid-fifties told us that it had given her a new lease of life. Heads seem to value these teachers very highly, the only criticism we heard was that 'they tend to push the reading a bit', due to their early experiences.

Once the mature teacher has decided to try to organize an integrated day, there seem to be four main points where adaptation is found particularly difficult:

1 Supervision of a variety of activities running simultaneously. This is a difficulty for all teachers but the experienced formal teacher, who is accustomed to knowing throughout the day exactly what each child is doing finds this particularly hard. In general, teachers learn to try various ways of organizing and experiment with the plan of the day to suit the children's needs. Mostly they also keep running records of what the various groups of children are doing on a postcard or notebook in the pocket, on a paper pinned to the wall or the teacher's table, or train the children to keep their own records on wall charts or in folders (see Chapter 9).
2 Using space to the best advantage. Teachers who have been accustomed to rows of desks with their own place in front of a blackboard, find difficulty at first in arranging a room as a workshop with no particular focal point. Mature teachers here are often helped by the headmistress and other teachers with experience of running the integrated day and they often show themselves very willing to experiment and change the arrangements of the room. There is really no other way to learn.

3 Working against external noise from practical areas. The general advice is to learn to disregard it while ensuring that it is a 'working noise' and not an undisciplined, time-wasting noise.
4 Keeping a check on individual children:
   1 Against loss of time. Teachers seem to find it helpful to have stated check-up periods during the day. Running records (see 1 above) are also helpful. As the teacher gains experience of each particular class, she learns to know those individual children who find settling to work very difficult, while she realizes that other children are 'trusties' and after the original stimulus can work without supervision. This helps to reduce the job to manageable proportions.
   2 To ensure progression. The mature teacher realizes the time difficulty of getting round to see each child, while there is also a tendency to lose sight of children in an open-plan area. The experienced teacher seems to meet this difficulty by planning her work very carefully and in some detail, so that children have planned for them teaching or apparatus that will move them on to the next point at just the right time.

The mature teacher usually adapts best to the integrated day by progressing at her own speed and in her own way. Participating in the school learning situation, instead of being shut away with her children in isolation in her classroom, she becomes aware of both her own capabilities and limitations and then can give help or alternatively seek help from colleagues. We found that the best teaching arose where the experienced teacher gave up the desire to remain 'king of the castle' in splendid isolation.

In the integrated day situation the kind of atmosphere created by teachers is of basic importance. This atmosphere is based on a calm stability and mutual acceptance which can then develop into one of the basic needs of childhood — a stimulating, adventurous environment.

For this environment to be achieved, it has become apparent that each teacher needs to develop her professional potential in four main fields. She needs to:

1 develop skills, imagination and knowledge to realize the scope of the children's interests and activities
2 understand children and their developmental sequences, in order to recognize the individual needs of each child

3 be a good organizer, collector of material, and coordinator of ideas
4 be able to provide for an ordered progression of work.

Children need to feel the security of a teacher who knows what she expects from them. This requires not merely consistent discipline and a planned progression for each activity but a continual assessment of three factors:

1 The ultimate aim of education as seen by the school and by the teacher herself.
2 The teacher's aim for each child, both long and short term (see Chapter 6).
3 The standard of the class.

Schemes of work, which suggest standards appropriate to each class in the school, help teachers by giving them a sense of direction and a knowledge of their part in the pattern of the school. They are usually supplied by the head and contain a basic scheme of what is expected in each subject or activity so that all can fit in. If no such scheme is supplied, it is proper for the teacher to ask for one. Where no scheme is forthcoming, the teacher can only bring the matter up in staff discussions or, notebook in hand, approach her colleagues. In an open plan school with free child and teacher movement, the overall aims are more readily assimilated and the standards of work correlated in action, but in more closed organizations these need continually to be restated by each teacher.

Chapter 6

CHILDREN IN THE INTEGRATED DAY

For many years it was a widely held and frequently stated view that school should prepare children for 'life' and that this 'life' was the life of work. Children were to be taught to 'work' by learning to perform efficiently tasks selected, set and supervised by the teacher. This authoritarian concept of education has been quietly eroded by the progressive primary schools, partly on the grounds that dictatorial education is no training for democratic participation and partly on the psychological basis that learning is an active process which requires full pupil involvement. This gradual revolution is now edging its way towards secondary education, explosively in 'pupil-power' movements and more persuasively in such writings as the Schools Council Moral Education project booklet, 'It is widely recognized today that a very real social need exists for pupils in secondary schools to learn how to practise democracy.' As the *Education Guardian* (June 20th 1972) suggested:

> The discussion now centres on breaking down the barriers between school and community . . . and on deciding where, if anywhere, the principle of pupil participation and choice logically stops. All these reforms have one single aim — to develop individual autonomy. Schools . . . must change radically and quickly in a democratic direction if they are to remain relevant to society in the seventies.

Teachers in integrated-day schools, while seldom specifically mentioning training for a democratic society, assume that this type of organization furthers the development of those qualities which writers on education see as essential to the democratic way of life. Infant or 'first school' teachers talk about the need to preserve and develop the child's individual autonomy, his need to be taught to make decisions and to act on them, to choose his own directions of interest and to be self-directing in following them. At the same time teachers stress the need for helping each child to see himself as part of a group, sharing ideas, materials, living-space, becoming aware of the needs of others and taking responsibility for communal property and activities. These attributes are seen as the foundation on which a satisfactory life-style in an adult community can be built. They are also seen as a lead-in to the educational pattern of the more progressive secondary schools in the county and to the way in which secondary education in general seems to be developing.

In practical terms, we found that most teachers taught the children the concept of 'us' and 'ours' rather than of 'me' and 'mine', so that they began to realize that, as everything at school is shared by everyone, they must all be prepared to take their share of responsibility. The visitor is invited to 'Come and see our puppet show; read our project book; look at our wall picture', to which is often added, 'I did this bit (of the whole)', i.e. this is *my* contribution to *our* effort. Quite young children begin to see themselves as part of a vigorous communal life even where, with the modern tendency to destroy communities in favour of slum-clearance or the motor-car, school is the first and only place where they can experience community belonging. We found that teachers spent time and care in discussion periods, helping the children to pinpoint the jobs that need doing to maintain the community, in devising ways of sharing these jobs equally while seeing that each child gets a varied experience of carrying out different kinds of jobs. In an integrated day, and especially in open-plan schools, a great deal of tidying-up, sorting and checking is needed and in the infant or first schools children are led to see the necessity of taking responsibility for maintaining rooms and materials in an orderly condition. A vital part of the child's training is that he should be made aware of the fact that other children must also share the apparatus and that he must leave it ready for the next child who wishes to use it and not simply abandon it when he has finished his own activity. Children like an orderly classroom and will readily undertake the work of sweeping-up, caring for flowers, plants and pets, checking library books, washing painting equipment, writing menus for meals, tidying boxes and shelves and generally keeping their room pleasant and habitable.

In many classrooms lists of jobs are kept, sometimes printed by the teacher and sometimes written by the children. Sometimes jobs are allotted by the class and sometimes chosen by the individual child. They may be changed every day or kept for a week or a month. As the children become accustomed to living in a community, they become aware of jobs that are well done or of jobs that have been neglected. 'Elizabeth is ever so good at taking in library books but Ann chatters too much and I can't work with her,' said an eight year old girl. 'John, you've not fed Bumper (the rabbit). He's banging his bowl,' said a six year old. And so the children begin to help, support and criticize one another and develop a feeling of community responsibility.

We found that most integrated-day teachers, when planning their work, allocated a definite time to tidying-up and arranging the room, so that jobs were not rushed and real training could be given. Many teachers deliberately focussed the children's attention on doing their jobs in pairs so that they learned to cooperate with one another. In one school, classroom discussions on alternate Monday mornings centred on the work to be done in maintaining the communal environment. Children who could write, each copied out a few of the jobs on separate pieces of paper, and these slips were pasted onto a large sheet of paper which was hung on the wall. Beside each job the teacher stapled an envelope and each child put his name-card into the job-envelope of his choice. There were usually enough jobs to enable the children to work in pairs; threes were seldom found to be a success.

As every teacher will know, although there is a school 'atmosphere', each group or class also has its own particular ethos. In authoritarian schools, this ethos is largely determined by the teacher *vis-à-vis* her pupils. She may be successful in enlisting their cooperation and have a very happy class or she may rely mainly on rules and authority, but the general pattern is one of pupils relating *to* a teacher in some pattern or other. In an integrated-day situation we found that the atmosphere tended to be one of working *with* rather than relating *to*, and this was always the ethos for which the teacher was striving. It is at least arguable that this atmosphere of working together, of support by the teacher for the autonomy of the pupils, is a basic grounding in democratic living on which teachers of older children can build in a more fully-conscious fashion.

Each child must be quite certain of the standards of behaviour and work which are expected of him. In the integrated day, the standards are clarified partly by class discussion but also by the experience of daily, free contact with other children and adults, through which the child can be helped to learn self-discipline and increase his awareness of the needs of others while gradually developing self-reliance.

In every society, each child has to learn to adopt a workable code of behaviour to maintain his position in the community. In a formal classroom children who had no option but to listen to the teacher often learned to adopt the acceptable code of appearing alert and interested while abstracting their secret thoughts into a private world. Among young children there was also a considerable amount of tale-bearing because the code was entirely the teacher's and this was thought to be a way of making oneself more acceptable to authority. 'Please, Miss, Timmy swore,' meaning 'He's bad, I'm good. Love me most.' Integrated-day teachers say that tale-telling has almost disappeared except in cases where the teacher's support is genuinely needed such as against individuals who habitually leave work-places untidy. Where the organization is freer, fussers can be met in a way that trains independent action. 'Please, Miss, he's got my chair — or my pencil,' receive the answer, 'Look round and take another,' instead of the piece of authoritarian discipline necessary when every child had his own private seat and pencil.

As in adult democracy, success depends on the ability to communicate and this involves two factors: the ability to speak and convey meaning, and the complementary ability to listen and receive meaning. Teachers certainly see the integrated day as a prime means of extending children's spoken language through social contact. Free movement and natural groupings mean that each child can meet more children more often, and also communicate with more teachers and a larger variety of adults. Older and younger children mingle and most gain in confidence and naturalness. Whereas under formal teaching the aim of the teacher was to keep her class silent so that the children could all listen to her teaching, in the integrated day teachers foster meaningful communication, keep records of social interaction and become concerned about the child who does not speak to others. As one mother put it, 'In Miss Wakefield's class, Michael spent nearly the whole of his first term in the corner because he would comment on what was going on. But before he went to school, he had always been with me and I had taught him to talk about what he did and saw. But now he is at North Leys School, he is learning a lot more because they do interesting things and he is encouraged to discuss them with the other children as he does with me.'

Just how important verbal communication can be in the development of children has been brought out by the work of Professor Bernstein in England, and Luria and Yudkin in Russia.

One of the most inhibiting factors in the interrelationship of teacher and child, or child and child can be the child's inability to communicate or express himself. He may come to school from a home situation which has never encouraged this self-expression and communication so that he lacks the necessary vocabulary or confidence. Such a child presents a special task to both teacher and other children. He needs both specific language teaching and opportunities for absorbing language from other children. An example of the degree to which verbal ability relates to socio-economic status was obtained when the seven year old classes of two adjoining local schools were tested on the Holborn Vocabulary Test. On one side of a main road, school A drew from a middle-class area of owner-occupied houses, on the other side, school B drew children from a slum-clearance housing estate. The highest score on vocabulary in school B was found to be equal only to the lowest score in school A, indicating what a tremendous disadvantage was being experienced by the school B children when they needed to express ideas, clarify thoughts or make decisions. School A children excelled every time in their ability to communicate, discuss and decide.

Of equal importance in communication is the need to ensure that children listen accurately so that the ideas of others can be evaluated. In formal teaching, children certainly are required to listen but as there is seldom any genuine pupil-participation required, the function of listening is largely absorbent and uncritical. When teacher has finished, children can often be heard asking, 'What did she say?' as though obedience to command or reproduction of received wisdom was all-important. In the integrated day, children find it necessary to listen to other adults and children, to understand what is said and either to accept or reject it with convincing reasons. For example, a child draws a picture of a bulldozer. 'This is a bulldozer.' 'But it's not right. It wouldn't go over bumps.' 'Yes it would. Why not?' 'Those tracks go much further along than that. They have lots of wheels inside, not just two.' 'Oh!'

Teachers in integrated-day first schools do not talk about training for democracy, but they talk a lot about the need to establish various forms of conduct and certain attitudes because character training has always been part of the way in which we see the educational process. The objective of an infant school or first school, according to these teachers, is to help children towards an autonomy which includes responsibility, self-discipline, sharing and cooperation. These traits may be thought important for our democratic way of life.

Again to quote *The Guardian*, 'The development of individual autonomy implies the mastery of certain basic skills like reading and writing which are the tools for autonomy in our society.' These tools, with other important skills, have to be learned and it is one of the tasks of schools to teach them. At one time, or nowadays in formal schools, the teacher decided when the child was ready to begin to learn literacy and numeracy, selected the reading scheme and taught the children in a series of graded lessons. Sometimes this was organized for the whole class, often it was group teaching, sometimes each child progressed at his own pace. But it was the teacher who made the decisions. In the modern primary school, and particularly integrated-day schools, we found a radical change in attitude from one in which the child is the passive recipient to one in which he is the active participant, while the teacher's function is to facilitate learning initiated by the pupils. The emphasis lies on placing the child in a rich, stimulating environment and fostering active exploration. Instead of quiet, biddable children, integrated-day schools hope to encourage alert, experimental attitudes, children full of curiosity and wonder, actively involved in choosing and developing their own learning — in psychological terms, children who are self-motivated. For example, Susan was making a poster to advertise a class play for assembly. 'My os won't come round, one side is flat,' she grumbled. 'If I show you how to do them and if you practise you could get them perfect,' said her teacher. One hour and about sixty os later, they were perfect and the poster was continued to Susan's satisfaction. This is a different form of motivation from 'Susan, your printing is good except for your os. Do them like this and practise six for me.'

In the integrated, open-plan situation children have the opportunity of seeing the next stages in their work being attempted by their peer group which often whets curiosity or acts as a spur. 'What's a perimeter? John and Neil were talking about the perimeter and it sounds nice.' 'Can I learn counting in twos?' 'Why?' 'My brother is learning and it sounds interesting.' 'Can I make a doll like Claire, only black?' Sometimes children learn almost unconsciously from work done by other groups. A little girl of five went home, word-perfect in *The Ballad of Semmerwater*. Her mother protested to the school that the child was too young to be taught such a poem but it became clear that she had learned it only by paying attention to the learning of a much older group of children. The sight and sound of other groups actually tackling new work and using different materials, cards and apparatus can be immensely stimulating to some children. It must be remembered, however, that young, intelligent children can sometimes be alarmed by the prospect of future problems. Richard, aged five but with a reading age of twelve, burst into tears when he saw some of the books the best seven year olds were reading. 'They are such big, thick books,' he said, 'they'll take too long. I'll never do it.' Other children, who perhaps initially lack confidence, can feel inadequate when they see the superior achievements and productions of older children. So although most teachers we met stressed the advantages of children seeing the next stages of their work done by older or abler children, a note of watchfulness was also sounded.

However, teachers also seem to feel that the integrated day makes it easier for each child to experience a sense of achievement. As children work individually or in groups and not all together on the same activity, standards of achievement are not so obvious nor are difficulties as pointed. Slow-learning children do not stand out as glaringly as under formal or group-work systems where children worked on 'the top table' or 'the bottom table'. Even when these groups were called 'blue' group or 'daisy' group, if grouped by ability children were soon able to crack the code. How competitive this kind of organization made children is exemplified by the statement of a boy about his friend. 'He's got one more boy to beat and then he'll be the best in the class.' We found that integrated-day teachers seldom grouped children by ability, except temporarily for a particular teaching point, but rather encouraged their children to form natural groups according to interests or deliberately grouped them to include a cross-section of ability.

This encourages children to pay attention to the diversity of talents and the problems of individual children in a more sympathetic way. 'Yes, but Gary finds maths hard,' said a child of another's sparse mathematics book. 'Send Paul, he always looks cheerful,' suggested the class members of a rather backward boy, when a messenger was required. Most teachers seem to encourage the children to work for their own personal satisfaction and build up a personal standard of achievement but this is easier where a child has an individual gift or bent or attractive characteristic. There are some unfortunate children for whom it is undoubtedly difficult to build a satisfactory personal image and who are rejected by almost all their contemporaries, although the integrated day is felt by teachers to offer the best chance of developing some kind of positive self-image in these children by watching for any sign of ability in any direction. The story told by A. S. Neil of one such child was mentioned by a teacher. He discovered the boy to be the champion spitter of the class and used this foundation of approval by his fellows as a base for educational achievement.

We found that teachers generally were aware of the problems of slow learners and the benefits to them of the integrated day. The group of specially gifted children seemed to us to pose problems that have perhaps not been so generally considered. Some teachers felt that it was only necessary to provide material and to allow these children to progress at their own rate but this philosophy seemed to us to raise other difficulties. A child who is unusually gifted may have worked through the whole of the available infant or first school material for some time before he is able to proceed to the junior or middle school. What then is the teacher to do? Is the child to mark time, becoming bored, lazy or 'naughty'; or is he to be allowed to proceed with the work commonly undertaken by the second school, thereby producing problems for the future? There is the case of Mark who, aged five, brought to school his eight year old brother's arithmetic exam paper, worked it 'for fun' and got it all right. When the teacher remonstrated that he did not know how to work division, he replied, 'Once I asked you what ÷ meant and you told me, so it's easy.' Or a boy of six who grumbled, 'I don't know what I am going to do till I'm seven because I've read every book in the infant school.' Or the five year old son of a biologist who read fluently and at home helped his father with real experiments and observations. He thought the infant school was simply silly and either refused to attend or if forced, was exceedingly naughty, although the school worked an integrated day and the teacher did her best to provide individual programmes for him. Another very brilliant child refused to cooperate in any way. As the headmaster told her parents, 'She simply sits like a pudding.'

We found that there were two main dangers for these exceptional children: they may easily see that they are outstandingly advanced for the class and react in several different ways, becoming bored, seeing no reason to make an effort or alternatively becoming nervous about their difference from other children and wanting to deny it. Schools which use family grouping or team teaching say that they do not find these children a problem until they go beyond the level of the other advanced children in the group, but somewhere in the last year or so of the first school these children represent difficulties for teachers. Gifted children may also feel unstimulated and lack companionship at their own level.

We have met various attempts to provide for the needs of this small but important group of children. In a few schools, the head gathers all these children together for one half-session every week, to organize some form of project at which they can work individually or in a group during the week as well as joining in the various activities of their own class. Another school encourages such children to listen to a particular school broadcast for older children and work on that for part of the week, finding that scientific or language programmes often interest these children. There have also been attempts to gather gifted children from neighbouring schools together for certain periods each week so that they may be helped to challenge and stimulate one another and really deploy their potential. Sometimes these groups have been run by students in colleges of education or university departments of education as part of their course. One LEA at least is experimenting with a special school for highly endowed children.

These are the children who are all-round gifted children but there are those whose gift takes one direction only such as music, dancing or art. These children are often found to be easier to cater for. Music and dancing are talents that need early training; a child's future may be impaired if nothing is done until the secondary stage. Many heads told us that in such cases they interviewed the parents to see what could be done and to make them aware of their child's talent. Where the parent could not afford outside tuition, musical heads have been known to give an unusually gifted child piano lessons, either in school time or directly after school, and with the parents' permission, have been successful in finding free pianos for home practice. One such head said of a six year old boy, 'He opened the sitting-room door and saw the piano. He didn't say a word but just walked over, sat down and played it as though it was the most natural thing in the world that he and a piano should come together.'

Sometimes a school will organize a special music or dancing class once a week for gifted children and try to arrange some practice time on the school premises. Some authorities organize art centres to which gifted children can be recommended. We found heads in general aware of this problem and usually ready to tap any source of help for the unusual child whose parents could not provide extra training for it. The general feeling was that special aptitude was more readily recognized in the loose organization of the integrated day than under more formal teaching. There was the nine year old girl who, when the teacher was humming and singing for a group rehearsal said, 'Shall I play it for you, Miss?' 'Can you sight read?' 'I can read that. Which key would you like it in?' One wonders if her ability would have been discovered in the formal singing lesson. An important byproduct of the integrated day is that it gives alert and sympathetic teachers the opportunity to discover unusually gifted children and help to make arrangements to satisfy their unique needs.

Although teachers who were working the integrated day commented mainly on its advantage to the children, they did not see these advantages as coming automatically and they were also aware of certain disadvantages that might accrue if the teacher was not alert to the possibilities. Some found that quiet or timid children might well be lost in the general activity, retreat from the situation and become passive followers. In the case of shy new entrants this is a distinct possibility. Many children come to school with preconceived ideas of a formal learning situation and are alarmed by informality. There is so much to learn, how to find materials, how to share, whom to work with, when to settle down as a group, that some children can develop a positive fear of freedom if not adequately helped. In integrated-day schools with a vertical or transitional grouping, new children are often only admitted, a few at a time, during the second week of term, when they will enter a settled, working community. The members have time to get to know each small group individually and the teacher can devote much attention to them specifically.

It is easy for a teacher to miss out on an important stage or point if she is overbusy with a group needing much attention. For example, we saw a group who were making models from junk in an area behind a screen. One child, who could not find exactly the three-dimensional material he wanted, cut his model out of flat cardboard very unsuccessfully, was most dissatisfied and threw up the whole idea because the teacher had not observed his difficulty in half an hour, and she had trained the children not to interrupt when she was teaching a group. Of course, total frustration was met equally in formal teaching when a child 'couldn't do his sums' and got them all wrong, but it is a point to watch in the integrated day.

It is also possible for certain children to become too dependent on other children. There is always someone to ask so they don't listen or think. Like the boy who came home and said that the teacher wished them to see a certain film at the cinema. 'Of course you can go. Which cinema?' 'I don't know.' 'Which film?' 'I don't know. I'll ask Robert' — who was away for the weekend and so no film was seen though Peter began to get the idea that some independent listening was required. Children from an unstimulating home may be willing to remain stuck at a stage in which they feel confident unless the teacher grasps the position and makes special provision so that the children move on to more profitable fields. Such children may look happy and busy and only careful examination of the content of their activities will reveal that they are actually wasting time.

As well as these groups of children who may need particular attention in the integrated day, teachers identify other categories of children who need special care. All classes are likely to have a cross-section of children who find great difficulty in the integrated day by virtue of its flexibility and the fact that many children are working individually, often away from the classroom. These categories of children have been helpfully described by one observer in the following terms:

1 *The wanderers*, who drift around from group to group or area to area, talking to their friends, looking at work in progress, seeming interested but never actively involved in anything. Some wandering children may be 'lost in space' not knowing the exact location of materials or work areas, others may be 'lost in time', confused between morning and afternoon, not sure if they have had dinner or not. Teachers who keep careful records of their children's activities soon identify these wandering children and plan to check up on their whereabouts at intervals while providing them with a definite programme of activities, which is periodically checked throughout the day until a more settled attitude is established. Usually teachers find it important to discover their interests, however rudimentary or ephemeral, and try to build on these. It has also been found helpful to try to establish such children to work in the company of responsible, settled children or else to keep them working alongside the teacher for some time.

2 *The abusers*, who activate madly but never clear up unless they are seen by the teacher, so that nothing is ready for the next children who come to the activity. The teacher who watches and records will soon discover these children and discussion periods can help to build up a group attitude about the need for leaving work

ready for the nextcomer, but the children may also be encouraged to tackle the untidy children for themselves. A child who succeeds to a messy or untidy work place can often be shown that he should find out who is the unhelpful one and ask him to clear it up. If altercations ensue, the teacher has the responsibility of sorting things out. This is one of the cases where an appeal by a child against untidiness can hardly be construed as tale-bearing but rather as a justified demand for support.

3 *The flitterers*, who move rapidly around from one activity to another, sampling everything in turn but persisting in nothing.

In young children, to whom the stimulating environment and wealth of opportunity is a new experience, this attitude of sampling is acceptable, but experienced teachers watch this point and expect that, by six years of age, children will be devoting much longer periods of time to their chosen activities and by seven they should be capable of really sustained effort. Those who do not show an increasing length of attention-span need special help. There are many possible causes of this flitting. Some children have never been taught to concentrate at home and others have never been allowed to concentrate, having been constantly distracted by adult help or interference. There are some areas where the children are mainly turned out of the homes to play in the street and never have a chance to settle until they come to school. For some children, the general level of work and activities is too high, for example Ian, who could only concentrate on nursery toys brought in specially for him to his six year old class. For others, the general level is too low or their special interest is not catered for like the doctor's six year old son who asked to bring his microscope to school and then wrote a long book about insects whereas before he had found nothing much to keep him gainfully employed. Some children need to be helped to settle and some need a firm hand if they are not to distract everyone else. Some need extending while for others the teacher must go back in time to find work suitable for a developmental level perhaps three years below their chronological age.

4 *The blasé*, who have done it all before and cannot find anything to do. However difficult such an attitude is for the teacher, it is, of course, not the child's fault. It can be a defensive measure against overpressure or overstimulation either at home or at school, and a chance for the child to idle and lie fallow for a time

may be just what is needed. However, some children actually arrive at school from rich, stimulating environments and may find the school a very poor exchange. They have in truth 'done it all before' and this is a challenge to the teacher's imagination and sympathy.

5 *The solitaries*, who get lost very quietly and cause no trouble to anyone although they may also contribute very little to the group. Some solitary children lack confidence and need to be 'shown' before they feel they can try the various activities, and need to be helped to make friends. But some children are genuinely solitary or 'introverted' by nature. They are happy pursuing their own occupations by themselves and feel little need for the companionship of others. It is a difficult and important task to distinguish between the natural, happy solitary and the frustrated, shy, artificially-made solitary child, who needs calm, friendly, reassuring help. In one class a naturally solitary boy of six, who always played happily by himself, watched a new student-teacher (also a solitary) for a few days and then quietly said, 'I know what you're like. You're like me. I shall tell you about my secret river.' In our Western society which tends to value extroverts and socialization, it is hard for teachers to decide whether to leave these children true to their own nature or to try to make them socialize. It is difficult to know which, in the long run, will make them happier. But naturally solitary children may well, in the end and in their own way, make a valuable contribution to life and one of the teacher's tasks is to get the other children to respect their personalities and appreciate their abilities.

6 *The town criers*, who shout and push their way through the various activities, always just out of the sight and hearing of their teacher. Such children are often potential leaders who shout loudly in order to get their 'better' ideas over and so dominate the game or group. These children may really have good ideas and a capacity for leadership but they need to be taught how to listen and consider the views of others, which is often very difficult for them. Group or class discussions in which all views are weighed up can be training for them. Such children can also benefit by being given definite charge of some project, making them responsible for bringing it to a successful conclusion by which they begin to learn that shouting, pushing and ordering are not enough, they have to enlist cooperation.

7 *The slow-coaches*, who take a long time to do anything. Slowness may be an innate quality which creates difficulties for the child as well as the teacher. Such a child needs sympathy and to be taught all the quick ways and short cuts available. He needs time for himself and patience from others. It is no fun for him to be always last in changing for PE, finishing his writing or putting on his outdoor clothes. Sometimes a mild degree of spasticity is involved. However, some children adopt dawdling as a defensive measure against demands that they do not wish to fulfil. 'I'll be as slow as I can,' was Linda's constant reply to any distasteful request. Others dawdle because they are mentally elsewhere, day dreaming. If these slow children are to get any value from the integrated day, teachers find that they must bear them constantly in mind and keep checking that a reasonable amount of work is in progress.

8 *The stickers*, who will keep on and on at one activity which they have already mastered and with which they feel safe. The first recognizable drawing of a child is often a house or a man. Some children will continue to draw nothing but the house or the man for weeks. This was the drawing that first brought them recognition and they see no reason to venture further. Sometimes one finds children who are content to write the first correct sentences (with picture) day after day. 'Last night I played with Simon and we played . . . Yesterday I went to the park and I saw . . .' And the changes are rung on the two items of news. These children often lack experience and need to have it extended together with the words in which such experiences may be described. They also need coaxing to attempt new forms of work or expression, and rather lavish praise and recognition when they succeed.

9 *The workers*, by whom we mean those children who tend to overextend themselves and perhaps get bogged down in one aspect of their development. Such children may be overambitious, over-perfectionist and anxious, like a girl of eight who wanted to make a grand Tutankhamen collage of all the objects shown in the exhibitions and had to be persuaded to select from all this material, something more within her scope. Another girl of six announced that she intended to write a book with a hundred pages. For three weeks she stuck at this task throughout each entire day but this only produced forty-eight pages and she had finally to be persuaded that full-page illustrations and patterned end papers

could help to make up the hundred pages she had set herself. As one teacher put it, 'These children need to be shown how to cut down on ambition.'

10 *The failures.* These children are almost more distressing to the careful teacher than they are to themselves except that they have to live permanently with themselves and the teachers do not. These are the children in whom nothing positive can be discovered, try as hard as one will. The other children avoid them. Every teacher who has encountered a 'failure child' will recognize the description. They are often plain, badly formed with poor eyesight or hearing, sometimes dirty, lethargic, often absent, clumsy, incompetent and unsociable. They are a great problem and it is difficult to know how to help them. They are probably even more conspicuous in the integrated day than in a formal situation. Some teachers try to find simple tasks that they can do which are skilfully arranged so that other children can admire the results. One teacher with a sad 'failure child' machined up a number of attractive but simple fabric animals and the child then cut up masses of old stockings and stuffed them. These were much admired by the rest of the class. Another such child was taught to work sewing cards and as these were provided for no one else, the other children coveted and admired these, too. But the teachers themselves felt very doubtful whether small successes of this nature had much real effect on the general depressed nature of the child's personality.

All classes everywhere tend to contain some of these various types of child. Teachers felt that these children both felt more difficulty and caused more trouble in the integrated day than in a more formal organization, by virtue of its flexibility and the fact that many children are working individually, often away from the classroom and the teacher. They said that, for certain children, some curtailment of freedom to choose was essential and often made the child feel more settled, secure and even more wanted and loved by the teacher because the teacher was making special arrangements for the child.

Teachers in general also stressed that it is important to see that each child has a try at everything provided over a period of time, and that children should be discouraged from narrowing their experience to a few chosen activities too thoroughly and too soon. Records must not only be carefully kept but equally carefully read over and interpreted so that the balance of any child's development over a period can be watched and, if necessary, corrected.

Recent television programmes, documentaries and newspaper articles have clearly shown that the main criterion by which the success of school education is judged by the consumers (i.e. children and parents) is its relevance to getting a job. But an increasingly technological society is also faced with the problem of using increased leisure. Teachers who work an integrated day believe that it gives them opportunities for basic training in important work attitudes such as self-discipline and the willingness to undertake a degree of drudgery in the pursuit of a self-imposed task. They also see the chance to give practice in the selection of self-chosen activities to fill untimetabled time.

Finally, it seems clear that among young people there is a growing movement towards cooperation and collaboration and away from competition. It is obvious that so long as our competitive society exists outside the school, no experiences within the school are likely entirely to do away with competitiveness, and children between the ages of seven and eleven are particularly engaged in competitive self-exploration. Yet the integrated day at least gives more scope than formal organization for developing social rather than individual attitudes towards work and so helps to move society in the direction in which it is tending to flow. It is encouraging children to learn how to use the stream rather than dam it up.

Chapter 7

RELATIONSHIPS WITH THE SECOND SCHOOL

In England there are several types of 'second schools', catering for rather different ages of children, which have evolved during our hundred years of state education. On the whole, the infant section of schooling has always been considered separately from the ensuing stages ever since, under Forster's 1862 *Revised Code*, infants under six were not required to be individually examined. The 'standards' were originally designed to begin with the six year olds, but were altered ten years later when the original seven year old Standard 2 became Standard I and the teachers of the under sevens were only required to display competence in class-teaching and show 'a cheerful and orderly set of pupils'. Schools, even small village schools, were built with separate rooms for the infants, attached to the 'all standard' school for boys and girls. It was not until 1931 after the Hadow Report that the 'junior school' began to emerge as a separate entity, and often it had to fit its new existence into buildings intended for the old 'all standard' school from which the 'seniors' had departed, sometimes taking its 'infant school' with it but sometimes leaving the infants behind in their 'infant' school. Primary education as we know it did not emerge until after the 1944 Act provided 'secondary education for all' and, for some years after the war ended, was necessarily contained in the various kinds of buildings from which the 'senior' children were departing for their new secondary schools, an exodus organized at different speeds by different LEAs throughout the country. As a result, many different forms of primary education were developed according to the buildings available and there are many different meanings to be attached to the term 'second school'.

In our area of Leicestershire alone we met five different kinds of second school and these varied in structure according to the way in which the primary stage was organized.

1 All-age, one-teacher primary schools with children aged five

to eleven followed by a second school which in this case is a secondary school on a separate and often distant campus. This basic type of school organization is disappearing rapidly in favour of larger primary schools serving groups of villages.

2 Infant/junior schools under one head in one building, with the deputy or a teacher with a post of special responsibility in charge of the infant classes if the school is large enough. The 'second' school in this case is the secondary school.

3 Infant schools followed by junior schools under separate heads but housed in two wings of the same building, using the same administrative facilities and sharing some specialist staff. Here the 'second school' is the junior school although the children only transfer from one part of the building to another.

4 Infant schools to seven years followed by separate junior schools for children aged seven to eleven. These schools may be on the same campus or may be some distance apart. In some cases, the junior schools are fed by two or three infant schools, each of which has its own head and distinct way of working. The 'second school' is again the junior school but geographically more remote from the infant schools than in the first three types.

5 What are now technically known as 'first schools', containing children from five to eight years, followed by 'second schools' for children of eight to eleven or twelve years.

It can be seen that first schools may contain children of five to seven, five to eight or five to eleven (not including nurseries) and that second schools may include children of seven to eleven, eight to eleven, or eleven onwards. First and second schools may occupy the same building or be quite widely separated. Second schools may be called junior, 'second' or even middle schools. There is no set pattern. To avoid confusion in this chapter we will simply call them 'second schools'.

All children, except those attending schools in categories 1 and 2, experience change in schooling before they reach the secondary stage and even those in category 2 schools experience some change, i.e. they are now called juniors instead of infants, have more direct contact with the head, a different timetable, more 'subjects' and often different methods of working. We have met heads who rarely entered the infant section of their own school and knew nothing about its routine; here the children experienced a real change to a 'second school' when they moved across the hall to the junior classrooms. English education, then, has a tradition of breaks between one level of schooling and the next. But whenever there is a change of school, there is a need for teacher awareness to help the children make a smooth transition from one school to the next. Variations in the planning and use of buildings mean that some groups of teachers need to make more effort to obtain an organic relationship with the second school than is required by others. Schools which share buildings, perhaps with some shared facilities, find contact simple and the children generally make an easy transition. In different buildings on the same campus, cooperation becomes more difficult but where schools are on different sites and geared to different catchment areas, then contacts between staff will not occur naturally and opportunities must be deliberately made if any form of positive relationship is to be built up.

The benefits of cooperation between first and second schools seem to us reasonable and obvious. Children themselves usually look forward to moving on to their second school however much they are enjoying their first. It is a status symbol, a sign of growing up. If the first school can reinforce this attitude in an intelligent way, both schools benefit but more particularly the second school. Where first and second schools cooperate in forming a relationship, the transition can usually be smooth for children, even where the basic methods are not the same. In cases where the second school uses formal methods while the integrated-day organization obtains in the first school, provided that the heads are quite clear about the work and aims of the other school, a reasonable transition can be worked out. Some first schools, for example, spend the children's last term in preparing them for the new system of working by organizing a project under some title such as 'getting ready for the next school'.

Perhaps the clearest way of emphasizing the need for cooperation is to show some of the results of noncooperation between first and second schools. Happily, we have found that heads are really becoming more appreciative of one another's work and less ready to stake claims to their own inviolate kingdoms, while local authorities are making the task of developing relationships easier by their attitudes to siting buildings, deployment of staff and establishment of teachers centres. However, some second school heads still run their schools in total isolation from what has gone before or what will come after. Some of the results of this policy that we have seen are:

1 The second school taking all children back to the very beginning of mathematics, teaching the children to count, sort, group and write figures as though nothing at all had been taught in the first school.
2 The second school trying to establish the children's level of reading without knowing the series of readers on which the children have been working and without any reference to the school records which have been sent to them. In the case of fluent readers, this probably does not matter since they can read anything but children who are still struggling with the mechanics of reading give a very false picture of their capacity, attainments and difficulties.
3 The second school repeating subject work which the children have already covered, for example, topics in science and techniques of instrumental playing in music.

All these unnecessary forms of repetition result in disenchantment and boredom for the children and in a time-wasting dissipation of keenness.

Some second schools, without consulting or even notifying their first schools, impose on the children a change in the style of writing, the type of writing paper (unlined to lined), writing implements (pencil to pen) or reading textbooks. The children are thereby presented with an extra set of problems at the time of transition and while some respond to the challenge, others are disheartened by the accumulation of difficulties. Such obstacles to progress may bear most hardly on the advanced, intelligent, lively children. We saw one school where children we had seen the year before writing pages of fluent, carefully spelled and punctuated stories in pencil were confined for over half a term to copying short sentences from the blackboard, 'in order to teach them to write on the lines'. The school seemed unaware that they could write at all.

Some second schools refuse even to consider, let alone learn and use, aids to reading adopted by the first school such as ita or Reading in Colour, even where the slower children have not reached the stage of transition to TO or black and white print. The obvious result is even greater confusion among those who are already finding reading difficult. In fact, some first schools had decided not to use ita because the second schools would not go along with it, even though they felt that the children would benefit by the method.

There is a very insidious danger where the second school arrogantly treats the work of the first school as 'baby-minding', ignores the first school or makes derogatory remarks to the children and their parents, telling the children, 'You are going to work now.' This total lack of comprehension of the values of self-direction and the difference between serious play and playing about depresses the status of teachers in the first school, both in the eyes of the children and the community. How many times has one heard parents of young infant teachers making such remark as, 'If you work hard, dear, perhaps they'll let you teach the bigger children.'

We also found second schools where the record cards, showing the children's handicaps and difficulties, were ignored and the school had to discover them all over again. This contemptuous attitude towards the work of colleagues resulted in vital time being lost in the children's development and in dealing with handicaps.

Looking at some of the results of isolationism, 'empire-building' and noncooperation, it is needless further to stress the point that cooperation between first and second schools is both sensible and important. The main question is how to obtain such cooperation or, at least, communication. The first essential is one willing headteacher. Two willing heads produce excellent results almost immediately but even where one head alone is cooperative, much can be done by adapting one school to the demands of the other where the interests of the children demand it. Where it is the head of the first school, with an integrated-day organization, who is more inclined to collaborate, there can be a last transitional term or half-term to the methods of the junior school which, because it is forward-looking, usually engages the children's interest. Reading schemes, alphabets, formation of figures, can all be related to the choice already made by the second school. This may seem to some heads to be a lowering of their dignity and status but this must be weighed against the benefits to the children.

At the same time, such heads usually strive to set up some measure of communication with their opposite number, although in some situations this is far from easy. We found that in some cases first and second schools were over half a mile apart and that sometimes a first school was preparing children for no fewer than three separate second schools with very different methods of organization and attitudes towards education. In other cases, the second school was drawing its children from three different first schools, some of which worked an integrated day while the others were organized more formally. It is undoubtedly much easier for heads to collaborate where they share the same building or have separate schools on the same campus. In such cases we frequently found that heads met daily for consultation during their coffee breaks and, where the same administrative staff was common to both schools, also met together over all kinds of work projects in the administrative rooms. In schools that share the same building the staff sometimes, but not always, had a shared common room which promoted interschool discussion and cooperation.

Where the two schools were separate, however, there were many interesting ideas aimed at promoting a good understanding between first and second schools. Some schools invite the staffs of the related schools for coffee or tea at stated intervals such as weekly or half termly. Sometimes they are just invited to drop in at any time but this may be less satisfactory on the grounds that a vague invitation is no invitation at all. An invitation to a whole staff needs a large common room, so sometimes a few teachers are invited at a time and the gathering is held in the hall. Sometimes staff are invited to discuss problems of mutual interest as well as to share a social occasion and such discussions may be opened by a speaker who is an authority in a particular field such as immigrant education or the teaching of reading. One infant school sponsored a series of weekly demonstrations for its own staff and the teachers from the junior school on the teaching of art, where the guest demonstrator was the art advisor to the LEA, a junior school arranged demonstrations in the making and firing of pottery by a member of staff who has specialist training in this field, while a teacher who bred tropical fish helped colleagues in both schools.

It is a commonplace for related first–second schools to invite one another to their concerts, plays, exhibitions and slide shows but some schools we found also issued invitations to the other school to bring concerts, plays or puppet shows across to their hall, thus providing children and teachers with another chance to visit the sister school and a change of venue which recognizes their importance. For instance, one junior school habitually moves across to play its new music to the older infants at assembly time.

Sometimes we have found first and second schools working together on a joint project. An interesting example of this kind of cooperation arose when an infant school was able to get hold of several old telephones and had parents and a teacher with sufficient know-how to be able to rig these up as private lines on which the children in one school could speak to the children in the other. This activity resulted in a considerable amount of mutually agreed basic work such as evolving telephone directories, conditions for making calls, timing and methods of payment. Another pair of schools made a fishpond with the older children and staff digging out the pond while the younger ones grew plants to put around the edge, decorated it with shells and made articles for a little sale to raise money to stock the pond with fish. In some schools, children from the older infants will play instruments in the junior school band or orchestra. A paired infant and junior school, on the same campus, organize every year a mutual fund-raising effort known as the schools' *Splash*. The school grounds are opened to the neighbourhood, there are sideshows, sports events and competitions, all devised by the staffs concerned and run as a cooperative effort. The resulting large sums of money provide many kinds of extras for the two schools including a swimming pool and instruments for a music room.

The first school may, on occasion, also undertake work for the second school such as making cakes for special functions, growing seeds for the gardens, helping with the older children's play by making simple properties, making useful articles such as lunch mats. Inquiry at the second school will often reveal such small aids as would be acceptable and will give young children the thrill of being useful to their seniors as well as giving them practice in community spirit.

Many schools provide for the staffs and a proportion of children from the other school to visit open days, carol services, nativity plays and other special festivals. In some schools, the older children come across to the first school or vice versa to attend morning assembly on one particular day each week. We found it almost customary for the second school to come to the first school at Christmas time to see the decorations and sometimes the first school would repeat decorations for the older children that they had particularly admired.

The drawing-up of internal school record cards requires the cooperation of both heads if they are to be really useful and, if at all possible, both staffs should also join in working out a satisfactory format. There are other matters of mutual interest to be discussed such as the style of handwriting to be taught and the selection of school readers or mathematical equipment. Some pairs or groups of schools are successful in organizing combined staff meetings to discuss such topics though it must be admitted that these have been found to be most successful where the schools are at least on the same campus so that time is not wasted in travelling between buildings and overcoming parking problems.

It has also been known for the teachers at pairs of schools to put on talks about the organization of their work, either for one another or as a combined operation for parents' days. Where the first school works an integrated day, this has been explained to the teachers of the second school. When the integrated day has been running for some time, teachers of the second school have been invited, one at a time, to visit and see for themselves exactly what is happening. Later, meetings have been held to discuss criticisms or interesting points raised by the second school in the light of what they have seen or the experiences they have had in working for a year to two with children who started their education in the integrated first school. By this kind of cross-fertilization, second school teachers are enabled to correct their impressions of what an integrated day is really like and how the children actually work within this framework while first-school teachers hear some evidence as to how their long-term aims work out in practice.

To summarize what may be called 'the mechanics of co-operation', we have noted eleven different ways in which first and second schools try to secure mutual agreement and understanding:

1 Social invitations to coffee breaks or tea parties at regular intervals.
2 Invitations to share lectures, discussions or special skills and equipment.
3 Invitations to concerts, plays, exhibitions, open-days.
4 Invitations to give concerts, plays, puppet shows in the other school.
5 Combined work on joint projects.
6 Work undertaken to help the other school.
7 Visits to the other school's assemblies, carol services, nativity plays etc.
8 Visiting the other school on Open Days.
9 Meetings to draw up internal school record cards.
10 Combined staff meetings to discuss matters of mutual interest.
11 Talks and discussions about the organization of the two schools.

Teachers in many infant or first schools have experimented for some time with various ways of preparing their children for life in the junior or second school or ways of making the transition work more smoothly. Where there is little measure of agreement between the schools and the first school works an integrated day, some schools, as we have mentioned before, arrange a partial change-over of methods for the older children in the last few weeks of the summer term, so that they can become more accustomed to a formal set-up while still contained within a familiar environment. The formality can then be explained, in the interests of the children, as part of the process of growing up and moving on, regardless of what the teachers actually think of it.

Where there is some measure of cooperation between the two schools, the head of the junior or second school often visits the first school to see the children who will be transferring at work in their classrooms. He may meet them for a talk about the new school and sometimes meet the parents also. This contact is perhaps rather slight and formal but at least these heads have some real experience of what has been already provided for the children, and the children at least know the head as a real person in the new setting. Some heads go further and arrange for the children to be taken to see their new classrooms and meet their teachers so that each child has a fairly clear picture of the new environment before the long summer holiday intervenes.

Some schools, however, have experimented further in their efforts to make this transitional period less of a strain to the children. A few schools have tried letting the teacher of the top infant class move over with the children to remain as their teacher for the first year in the junior school. It has been found that this kind of organization has several advantages. The teacher knows the children; those who are just beginning to read suffer no check in their development; anxious children are helped over the first difficult stages; problems can be explained personally to the second school teachers. Moreover, the teacher acts as a kind of liaison officer between the two schools. She understands the working of both and can interpret each to the other. Where the first school is working an integrated day, she may act as an ambassador for this foreign way of working. She is on hand to answer questions, to listen to criticism and consider its justification, to explain, to mediate between the two systems. Where the second school also works an integrated day, she can learn much from experiencing her own type of organization used with other teachers and older children in a different setting. Naturally, much of the success or failure of this scheme depends not on the scheme itself, but on the personality, intelligence and discretion of the teacher who has to adapt herself to the philosophy and personalities of two separate schools in alternate years, without offending either. With the right teachers who are interested in the possibilities, this scheme has had much success.

Other experiments we have observed include arrangements whereby the first school arranges the class lists for the first year of the second school or sends up recommendations for keeping friendship groups together. It is often very distressing for children to find themselves not merely in a new school, but separated for some administrative reason from children with whom they have been friends since they first entered school. Again, some second schools arrange that the children shall bring their readers and work books along with them from the first school, and the children clearly understand that this will be so.

Looking around the schools, the general trend on all levels — administrative and educational — seems to be towards greater cooperation and more unity. Colleges of education are also altering their attitude towards specific training. Some now train for primary teaching as a whole instead of requiring students to opt for training as nursery or infant or junior teachers and confining their experience to these narrow age ranges. Before leaving college, many students are now encouraged to plan the early years of their career so that they teach for a few years in an infant school and then for a few years in a junior school, so that they have real experience of the whole primary spectrum. Students who have been encouraged to think in this way seem now to be making a significant contribution to the development of relationships between first and second schools.

Chapter 8

PARENTS AND OTHER HELPERS

Parents

Valuable as schools often are, teachers in general will agree that the influence of the parents is paramount in the child's life. In the earliest years, parents form the attitudes to social relationships and learning with which the child enters school and these attitudes are continually reinforced throughout his schooldays, since children spend more than three-quarters of their time in the environment created by the parents. If parental attitudes are at variance with those of the school, the child is almost always confused in his efforts to adjust and there is seldom much doubt as to which side will win in the end. This being so, it is very curious that until recently very little was done in England to forge real relationships between homes and schools or to help the parents understand what went on in the five, six or seven hours when the children were actually in school. One member of the investigating group recalls how shocked she was only twenty years ago, when she returned from West Africa, where parents had sat with their children in classrooms to learn English and hung over the walls of school kitchens offering advice in domestic science periods, to find notices displayed in English schools stating, 'Parents must not proceed beyond this line', and 'Parents must not enter this school without an appointment'. Such attitudes seemed not merely offensive in themselves but denied a great opportunity for educating and helping the parents at a time when they are most receptive as to what they can do for their children. They also prevented the school from receiving from parents the knowledge and help that they alone can give. For no one knows a child quite like its parents.

Slowly this attitude is changing to a realization that if parents need schools for some aspects of the education of their children, teachers need parents and have a duty towards them. We found that most modern headteachers want to make the parents feel useful, wanted and welcome in the school. In this new view of parents the integrated day has a helpful part to play, for the freedom and flexibility of its organization means that parents can feel free to visit the school at need and can also assume helpful roles in the daily work.

The knowledge that they can contribute to the children's school education seems, on the whole, to be appreciated by middle-class parents, even if they do not actually participate. They have tended to be afraid of approaching the school, diffident about seeming to interfere, anxious about making life difficult for their children by suggesting or complaining and thereby annoying the teachers though, of course, there is always a minority who thinks it knows as much about education as the teachers. When parents were kept out of school, none of these attitudes were ever tested. Often the middle-class parent is caught in a dilemma, wanting the child to succeed because failure is seen as future socio-economic disaster as well as a reflection on the parent, but at the same time wanting the child to be happy. Because schools have changed so much, parents feel no confidence in their ability to help their child, since all they have to offer is their recollection of the way in which they were treated in school and how they reacted, and these recollections are very subjective. Parents tend to remember parts of their education because they were specially nice, 'We sewed with coloured thread and played singing games', or specially nasty, 'We did nothing in arithmetic but recite tables', or merely repetitive, 'We spent hours pulling material to pieces to stuff a cushion'. They know that schools and methods are different now but do not know in what way. Nothing is taught to their children in the way it was presented to them. They do not understand the integrated day, which they see as a lack of discipline and ordered learning, and contrast it with an idealized recollection of children who sat quietly in desks learning all together from a teacher and a blackboard. All this leads to an undesirable hesitancy on the part of the parent in dealing with his child or to equally undesirable criticism to the child of what is going on in the school, as the parent understands it. The modern headteacher brings the parent into the school to see what is going on, explains the new ideas and methods, asks for the parents' help in teaching the child and gives guidance as to how this help should be given so that the middle-class parent's interest in his child's progress is used effectively and in harness with the school's methods of working.

Working-class parents, on the whole, have been found to divide into roughly two opposing types. Many see education as a key by which children can unlock a more secure, interesting or socially-advantaged future for themselves. These parents tend to be even more anxious than their middle-class counterparts; they may push their children harder and perhaps take a less realistic view of their children's abilities. On the other hand, they are often highly cooperative with the school, especially where the school serves a mainly working-class area. Where the area is socially mixed, working-class parents may tend to feel unnecessarily inferior and leave the more enterprising work or the organizing of committees to the middle-class parents. From these schools, heads told us that their parents would rather 'pop-in' for a chat than ask about their child at parents' days and this 'popping-in' is, as we have said before, greatly facilitated by an integrated-day organization.

Conversely, some schools in educational priority areas, mentioned parents whose attitude was one of quite simply not bothering, 'Oh, me duck, I couldn't do nothing like that when I was at school.' Such parents are often quite undemanding of any educational effort from their offspring. They tend either to push their children into school at an early age, often without accompanying them on entry and sending the child quite alone or with another child, or else they keep them dependent for longer than is customary with middle-class children. These parents tended to come to the school not to discuss their children's education, but to complain, to see the doctor and to get clothes or shoes for their children. When invited to look round the school, they come for the cups of tea and cake but can hardly be persuaded to look at their children's work.

It became obvious to us that ways of enlisting parental co-operation which were right for one type of school might not be successful with other kinds of communities, and we found the most effective parent-teacher contacts took place where the head had planned her strategy in relation to what she and her staff knew of the local parents. However, we found some changes in the planning of the new schools which are now often envisaged more as community centres than just schools. Early attempts put the local library on the school campus, to be used by adults and children alike both throughout the day and in the evenings. Many of the newer schools are now designed as real community centres, with special areas for adult education (instead of adults having to squeeze themselves into child-sized desks), rooms that can be hired by community groups (art clubs, wine clubs, chess or gardening clubs), facilities for health centres and libraries. Such all-purpose buildings accustom the community to visit the school and help to create the concept of 'our school'.

But in any kind of school building we found that staffs of schools could be successful in creating opportunities for relating to parents if they really felt the value of such relationships. Most schools organized on the integrated-day pattern encouraged and used casual contacts with the parents but many made definite time-tabled arrangements for parents to help in the schools on specified jobs or to teach groups of children particular skills. We found that some heads felt an obligation to help parents to educate themselves in their parental roles by providing classes in child care or the new methods of teaching, or by arranging a spare classroom or the school foyer as a parents' room for work and study. Many schools had Parent Teacher Associations but the ways in which these were organized were very varied, ranging from social or money raising events to parent-teacher discussion forums where ideas about running the school could be debated and pooled. Every school that we visited had some form of Parents' Day but the purposes and organization of these days differed very widely.

We shall now examine these four main approaches to parents in some detail.

Parents' work in schools

Timetabled arrangements with parents

The kind of help that parents can give of course depends on their degree of knowledge, enterprise and involvement. Many schools are able to enlist parents to visit on particular days to hear children read, read to children, talk with children who need extra practice or stimulus, take small groups for cooking, needlework, gardening or woodwork. Heads often arrange for a group of mothers to visit on one afternoon each week and, using perhaps the staff room or foyer or part of the hall, mend equipment, make costumes for plays or concerts, or repair library books. For example, we visited the Hawthorne School, where three parents give their time each Thursday afternoon in order to mend library books, catalogue the library and generally keep it in good working order. In addition, two parents are attached to each class to help the teacher in various skilled but nonprofessional jobs. They will copy music, make simple musical instruments and help children to make others. They write out work cards, sticking on pictures and covering them with waterproof plastic, and they will make work books for the children to use. These helpful activities are carried out either at school or at home, whichever suits the situation and the parent best. This school also has a small indoor swimming pool, set up in a spare classroom and provided by funds raised by the PTA. The parents provide help with teaching swimming to small groups and supervise the undressing and dressing of the children. Another feature of this school is that the mothers can also learn to swim and are given the same certificate of competence as their children. In a village school, one of the local mothers who is studying for her Cordon Bleu cookery examination teaches cookery to groups of children on Wednesday afternoon, while a canal-boat owner will take groups of ten children and a teacher on trips to study the geography and natural history of the canal system, and this is a regular engagement for the summer term. Another village school, with a field as part of its grounds, organized a fathers' club on Sunday mornings, who planted suitable trees, shrubs and wild flowers for local wild life, built the necessary hide-outs for observation and did the maintenance work to keep it in working condition. Schools have also organized fathers' evening clubs to build and repair wooden equipment for the children and to set up a school adventure playground.

Occasional work in schools

Parents may be asked to visit a school in order to give help for a particular event, such as the school sports day or a school visit. For parents living in an educational priority area, with little experience of working in a school, this may be an excellent way of beginning. For example, a school taking all its children to the local zoo for the day organized them in small groups, each attached to a mother who gave her services for the trip but paid at the same rate as the children for the outing, although there was absolutely no tradition of parents working in the school in any other way. Again, parents who have special knowledge which is attractive to children, such as footballers, policemen, fishermen, nurses, dog-trainers, are asked to visit schools to talk about their work where this is appropriate. Arrangements may also be made for parents with a special interest such as chess, stamp collecting or canal boats to talk to potentially interested children and teachers in order to start or develop an interest, or to get a club going among the older children.

Education in the parental role

Education for parenthood has long been recommended as a topic for the secondary school curriculum. In some schools it has actually been practised. Heads of progressive primary schools, however, seemed to find that the most fruitful time for such education comes when the adults actually have children and so become parents. They then become alive to the realities of the problems involved. Schools arrange to help parents in various ways, apart from the head making appointments for consultation or being around for informal visits. In some schools posters, books and other materials about child education are kept on display in any place where parents can readily see them, such as in the entrance hall or outside the head's room. Seating accommodation and a table are often provided so that parents, waiting to see the head or collect their children or attending their child's visit to the doctor, can study any material that appeals to them. Some schools encourage parents to come at any time to consult books or magazines. Where there is a children's library room, the material for parents may be placed in racks just outside, so that parents also have a chance to see the sort of books provided for their children which, it is hoped, will encourage them in wise buying. If there is no school library, selected books and materials for children may be placed in the entrance hall along with the books for parents. One school in an EPA turned a spare classroom into a room for the local parents whose children attend the nursery classes. The equipment included materials for making tea, a second-hand sewing machine and patterns of children's clothes, and simple pamphlets and women's magazines containing articles on the rearing of children.

In schools where parents give regular help, they are likely to pick up new ideas about things they can do with or for their children. In addition, schools often organize evening meetings where the parents have new methods (such as ita reading and Nuffield mathematics) explained to them in detail and are also given a chance to use the equipment. In this way they can really grasp what is going on in the school, feel confident about helping their children at home and become better able to talk intelligently with the children about what they are learning in school. Some heads also arrange with publishers to put on exhibitions of books suitable for children, which are particularly helpful to parents if held in October or November, when Christmas presents are being considered. Local libraries will sometimes make for the school lists of books particularly suitable for different ages and these can be duplicated for interested parents, but a list is not really as helpful as a chance actually to examine the books. Some village schools are open on Saturdays two or three times a year, and the parents are invited in to try out the art and craft material available to their children. Teachers will attend and the parents spend a whole day modelling in clay, printing papers and fabrics, painting or using junk materials.

One school is running a magazine for parents and includes in it information about new methods of teaching, or discussions of problems facing parents such as suitable amounts of pocket money, bedtimes, hard-wearing shoes and clothes, holiday interests for children etc.

Many schools organize a preschool entry class for one day or half-day each week. Children accompanied by their parents are invited to attend in the term before compulsory education starts. The aim is to accustom the children to school personnel, routines and to being with a number of other children, but there is a bonus in introducing parents, also, to the aims and methods of the school and what the staff feel they can do for the children. Some heads invite parents to open evenings so that the fathers can come after work. If a talk, film or discussion forum is arranged, all parents may be invited together but where the aim is to allow each parent to talk about his child with the teacher most responsible for him, half a dozen parents to each teacher may be invited on one of successive evenings, until all the parents have had a chance for a leisurely, informal chat about their child's progress. A few heads told us that they asked their teachers to pay an informal home visit to each child's parents at least once during the year and more often if the visit seemed especially welcome or valuable.

Schools in educational priority areas or areas where there is little tradition of school–parent cooperation, seemed to find it particularly helpful to invite parents to visit the school for definite, short occasions where they would see the children actually participating in some activity and so gain a new concept of their own child's abilities and how he fits into the community. Some schools give parents an open invitation to attend the morning assembly on a particular day in each week when each class takes it in turn to organize a special topic for the parents and the other children. Schools also invite parents to hear their children sing, act and play musical instruments in carol services, nativity plays and concerts and from such programmes parents can discover, sometimes for the first time, that their child is musically gifted, has a specially good voice, reads or speaks verse particularly clearly or is gifted in drama, for it is not until a parent sees a child with a large number of his contemporaries that she is able to evaluate his abilities and make provision for them.

Parent-Teacher Associations

Some of the integrated-day schools had no formal Parent-Teacher Associations. In some EPAS the heads said that they could not get the parents to attend and found informal meetings, open-access and occasional parental help, of the kind described in the last section, to be more successful in getting the parents into school. A few heads in other areas felt that they had such good contact with the parents through other means that a PTA was unnecessary.

Where PTAS exist, they seem to be organized for three main purposes:

1. arranging social functions
2. fund raising
3. discussing new ideas in education and the general running of the school.

Any PTA might have as an objective not merely one of these objectives but two or even all of them.

On the new housing estates, organizing social functions seemed particularly important since it helped the parents both to get to know each other and the school staff. In addition to the usual whist drives, concerts, dances, barbecues, film shows, cricket and football matches, we also found PTAS that organized their own newspapers, newsletters, sales of second-hand school uniform, carnivals, rounders matches, knock-out tennis tournaments, wine circles and wine tasting holidays, visits to London for exhibitions or theatres. According to the parents' interest and hobbies, PTAS can do much to develop a lively social life in a village or on a new housing estate and, where the parents are socially stimulated, benefit to the children will probably follow from the increased range of interests and social contacts developed by the adults with whom they live.

Fund raising to provide extra facilities for the children (swimming pools, animal houses, musical instruments etc), special treats particularly in more deprived areas (parties, outings, visits of a puppet or theatre group to the school etc) or large, expensive items of equipment (projectors, duplicators, potters' wheels etc) is the earliest and the most common activity of the PTAS. Most associations seemed to use the ordinary methods of raising money, such as rummage sales, bring and buy sales, concerts and entertainments. The newer idea of 'sponsoring' has been taken over by some PTAs. Children are 'sponsored' by the members and earn money for the PTA fund by the number of lengths they can swim, the number of times they can walk round the school campus, the amount of newspaper or silver foil that they can collect etc, these activities being supervised by the school but paid for by the members and friends of the PTA. Where a school has added facilities as a community centre, it is possible to hold coffee mornings. PTAs can also stimulate their members to provide for the school's needs in kind as well as money and many parents have donated quantities of useful but disused lines from workshops and factories (e.g. hosiery cones, cards of button samples, card or paper printed only on one side etc).

Meetings to discuss new ideas in education may be centred round a speaker who will present the new concept or a film which shows how it works in another area, or a panel or Brains Trust which has the advantage of presenting the innovation in a varied way according to the personalities involved. They may be triggered off by some new method which the school is using or by a controversial film or television programme which provokes parents into discussion. Sometimes PTAs will arrange discussion groups or even action groups in response to some aspect of official policy (e.g. the 11 + and comprehensive education, the closure or opening or siting of nursery schools etc) which is about to make an impact on the locality and affect the lives of parents and children.

Parents' day or open day

Most schools seem to have the customary 'day' when they are open to parents. This is usually organized so that the visitors can see their children working as well as examples of the work they have done during the year. Often there is an entertainment or display as well. However, we found some interesting variants of the 'open day'.

Some heads arrange for the open day to be held in the evening, so that fathers can come too. The school may be open for the evening only, in which case neither parent will see the children working though they may see some of the older children, invited to return to school after tea, giving a display of some kind. Other schools start their open day with the afternoon session, so that mothers and fathers who are not working can see their children's usual afternoon activities. The school then remains open during the evening. This makes a very long day for the teachers but, if it only happens once a year, the fatigue is usually willingly borne for the sake of the advantage to the parents. It is really important in deciding on the form the open day will take that the head should know the district thoroughly. As one head pointed out, an open evening would present problems in his area since most families had a changing succession of 'uncles' rather than real fathers.

Other forms of open day had quite different names and organization. Several schools organized a whole or half-day pre-school visit by the parents who were invited in small groups, bringing their children with them. The mothers then spent the time learning about the school and visiting their children's future classes, while the children were occupied in the nursery, reception class or the family group to which they would later belong. Where there is an integrated day, mothers are also often asked to stay for the whole of the child's first morning in school, only a few children being admitted each day at the beginning of the term so that the teacher has time for both parent and child.

One school had a tea-party for parents, who first arrived in the morning to help the children make the cakes, decorate the tables, arrange the flowers, write the place-names, etc. Another school had an art exhibition to which parents, teachers, school managers and ancillary staff were invited to contribute. Conceived as a simple one-day exhibition in a working-class area, the parents' response was so enthusiastic that the large hall was filled with work, beautifully arranged and labelled with official, duplicated forms that each parent filled in, and the show lasted for a week becoming a real focus for the community. It was most revealing to the teachers to see the unsuspected talents and interests of many of the parents. It also gave the parents a new view of the primary teachers among whom were rather unexpectedly found potters, painters, carpenters and embroiderers.

In making relationships with parents, teachers may perhaps find value in considering what kinds of information they hope to obtain and how it can be of use in their work. Most teachers felt that contact with parents broadened their understanding of the children. On the positive side they were able to see which children received help, stimulus and encouragement from in the home, use this in planning their work and help the parents further to understand and foster their children's interests and abilities. On the more negative side they were better able to understand how behavioural problems arose from family upsets and therefore deal with difficulties in a constructive way. Teachers also came to a clearer knowledge of the kind of discipline used in the home and could build on this with each child.

It is often good for children to see parents and teachers as one, for it gives them a sense of order, unity and security in their lives. Where teachers and parents have roughly the same values, this unity is fairly easily attained. But experienced teachers pointed out that some children go to school to find a world that is more to their liking than the home. When rather facetiously asked by the teacher, 'Why don't you go home? Haven't you any homes to go to?' two children replied, 'Yes, but we like school better.' And for some children, school and the teacher represents the best that life has to offer, their one glimpse of a wider, more sympathetic environment. In such cases, contact with the parent may pinpoint the difficulties that children are experiencing in reconciling home values with school values. In other cases, the teacher must be very wary lest she betrays the inner world of the child to unsympathizing adults.

Teachers also said that contact with the parents helped them to understand what the parents wanted of and for their children, and therefore the kinds of pressures that were exerted in the home, e.g. parents who aimed at their children passing the 11+ exam, at making their children responsible (often for younger siblings), at early literacy (particularly with boys who often find reading difficult). It was also helpful to know parental views about the child's future, e.g. those who would proceed to private schools, boarding schools, single-sex schools, ballet or drama schools. In addition, parents with children that they find difficult can often be helped and supported by teachers where there is sympathetic contact.

All this takes time and effort. As the Plowden Report states in a highly sympathetic paragraph:

> Much depends on the teachers. Teachers are already hard pressed and nowhere more so than in the districts where cooperation is most needed and hardest to win. . . . Forty children will seem enough to many, without adding eighty fathers and mothers. . . . Yet we are convinced that to make the effort will not only add depth to their understanding of their children but will also bring out that support from the home which is still often latent.

Ancillary helpers

We found that local authorities are increasingly supplying ancillary helpers. These helpers are neither trained teachers nor trained assistants but simply women of commonsense, goodwill and a reasonable standard of education. They are not employed to replace the teacher in any way but simply to give her more time for actual teaching by relieving her of routine duties such as mixing paint, making paste and cutting paper. With our increased knowledge of the importance of language in education, ancillary helpers are valued by teachers both as another pair of hands and another adult voice to aid in the learning of vocabulary and the art of conversation. Teachers may employ ancillary helpers in talking with individual children who need extra conversation, in reading a book with a particular child for enjoyment or stimulus, in talking with a small group or reading with them. Research has shown that too much reliance on other children for conversation seriously inhibits language development; the doubling of adult availability in a classroom situation gives the children at least twice the amount of conversational interchange on an adult level. The teacher has also more of her trained skill to devote to the development of the children. Where teachers' assistants are employed the teachers are freed from many routine jobs and their attention can be given to the task of organizing an environment suitable for the children to learn in and helping them to use it to their best advantage.

Students

Wisely-used, teachers find students both a stimulus and a help in working an integrated day. Like the ancillary helper, the student provides another pair of adult hands and ears and a further chance of talking with a grown-up. As students enter teacher training with advanced qualifications, the range of experiences they can offer the children widens. Many students now bring to the schools a working knowledge of foreign travel, a foreign language, guitar playing, rock climbing, pot-holing, canoeing, cross-country walking and map-reading, playing in groups or bands, running play-centres and youth groups, helping in archaeological 'digs' etc. As the teacher becomes aware of what her student has to offer, she can arrange the environment of the integrated day so that the children can take advantage of these new opportunities by working in groups or as individuals with the student. For example, a student with experience of rock climbing was able to increase the children's vocabulary and general knowledge by bringing his climbing 'gear' to school to be examined and discussed. He was able to tell the children stories of climbers illustrated with his own photographs and interest them in a series of programmes then being shown on TV.

There seem to be two sources of students. There are NNEB students who may visit the schools for two or three days each week. There are also teachers in training from colleges of education or university departments of education.

NNEB students we found usually helping the teacher in her routine work but also talking with individuals or groups who needed special attention. They also tell stories to small groups of children while the teacher is busy with the general supervision of the children working in the integrated day. At the end of the morning or the afternoon, we found that the NNEB student, as she became more proficient, would also take the whole class for story or poetry while the teacher could work with one or two children who specially needed her. NNEB students will help the children to do specially awkward bits of creative work and they are another pair of ears to listen to children's confidences or reading. As they are in college to learn the job of nursery teaching, teachers also found them a source of new ideas through their contact with other schools through their tutors.

Students from colleges or departments of education may be in the schools for a variety of reasons. We found that some colleges sent groups of students regularly into schools on particular days throughout the year. Sometimes the group came simply to learn and practise the general work of a primary teacher, in which case the students could be used as assistants in helping the teacher with her integrated day, or they might be given a group of their own for the development of a project. If the needs of particular children were explained beforehand to the college authorities, it seemed that they would usually cooperate in sending students who could help in areas of work that the teachers found difficult. For example, a group of students specializing in the teaching of reading would be attached to an EPA school or a school for immigrants where the reading is a particular problem.

Sometimes groups are attached to schools to practise the teaching of particular subjects at primary level. For instance, students taking environmental studies may work in primary schools one day each week for a term to gain practical experience which can prove very helpful to the regular teacher, if she organizes her work to make use of the opportunity. Where the students come in pairs or fours to a class, it is easier to take the children on profitable expeditions to see interesting environmental situations and then the teacher can provide follow-up material during the week. The students learn from the teacher how to use environmental material with the children, while visits are made richer by the increased number of adults.

Some colleges arranged for classes of children to visit and use their facilities each week. We saw classes of primary children in the college gymnasium, working in the dance studios or using the facilities of the art and craft department, helped by the subject students as part of their training. This extra stimulus was valued by the teachers, who accompanied their classes, and much useful follow-up work resulted. A particularly interesting example came when two schools, one with 80 per cent immigrants and one with no immigrants at all, combined each to send twenty children in need of special care and attention to the local college for one weekly half-day throughout the year. Each immigrant child chose a local child to work with and each pair was supervised by a student. There was a lot of spin off from this experience in both schools, each of which worked on an integrated day and could therefore arrange for suitable follow-up activities.

Teaching practice is seldom regarded by teachers as an unmixed blessing but, in the integrated day, what is lost in certain directions can often be regained by opportunities for the teacher to work particularly with certain groups or individuals while the student proceeds with the main body of children. Unless the student was very incompetent, we found that teachers on the whole welcomed the new ideas that they brought and found the help of another adult very useful. Teaching in an integrated-day situation is technically very difficult and we found that it led to a closer degree of cooperation between teacher and student, together with more true discussion and exchange of ideas, than was necessary in more formal schools.

Secondary school children

In some first schools, we found fifth-year secondary girls helping in various ways. Sometimes they had been sent by the local secondary school as part of a course for preparation for parenthood in which they learnt about the development of normal children, the kinds of toys and books suitable for the different ages and how to tell stories and rhymes. In EPA areas they might just be learning from the teachers how to talk to younger children and how to play. The free organization of the integrated day proved particularly useful to this kind of work, which was helping to forge a real bond between primary and secondary schools.

In the summer term in particular, secondary schools arrange with their primary schools for girls intending to take the NNEB course to spend some time trying out their aptitude for work with younger children. One secondary school regularly allows fifth-year nonacademic girls to help for a month each in the primary school as a means of giving them status and responsibility. The choice belongs to the girl, the primary school uses her on jobs from the ancillary workers' schedule and both schools report favourably on the experiment.

First schools have come a long way from the view that the teacher's classroom is her kingdom and that the place of all other adults is outside it. Increased knowledge of the power of language and the importance of environmental influences are leading schools to become more open and to forge links between themselves and the community. There are now in many progressive schools a great variety of adults and teenagers who visit the school to contribute what they have to give, and receive in return a greater share of responsibility for the education of the community's children.

Chapter 9

KEEPING RECORDS

Throughout this book we have emphasized repeatedly the importance which integrated-day teachers attach to recording. It is not merely the *keeping* of careful records which they find important but also their constant *use* in planning future work. Inexperienced teachers often feel that recording is an unnecessary chore, since they carry it all in their heads. But which experienced teacher has not been caught out by a request from a head, because of a parental visit, for factual information about some quiet, inoffensive, hardworking child whom she has hardly noticed for days beyond hearing the usual reading quota? And the exact development of a project, with all its individual ramifications, is soon forgotten when another interest arises. The freer the work, the more essential it is to keep track of the exact ground covered by each child within it, so that deficiencies may be made good and abilities developed.

LEA official school record cards

There are many kinds of records kept by first schools working an integrated day. Some are obligatory and common to all schools in an area; some are devised by the head and all teachers in her school are required to keep them; some are invented by individual teachers to further their own work. The record which is essentially common to all schools in a particular area is the local education authority official record, which is confidential and passed, with the child, from head to head as the pupil proceeds through the school system. Discussion about the format of the official school record is not really relevant in a book on the integrated day, since the one format has to fit all schools in any particular LEA, be they integrated or formal. However, these records are revised and discussed and teachers had several suggestions as to how they could be improved. Integrated-day teachers made three specific kinds of criticisms of LEA record cards. The main causes of difficulty appear to be as follows:

1 The record form dictates that information about the child must be organized under 'subject' headings, even where children have been taught under a free and integrated system. As one headmistress wrote, 'We need to break away from designs of record cards that require teachers to classify infants according to grades and to list their attainments under subject headings. In modern education so much work overlaps one subject with another that this is increasingly difficult and many of the subjects listed on LEA record cards are now taught far more incidentally and with other subjects, e.g. nature study which can involve mathematics, written English, reading, poetry, stories, singing, music and drama. Some record cards, moreover, stress the traditional three RS almost exclusively and ask for no report on children's artistic, musical or physical aptitudes and skills except obliquely under interests and disabilities or in a very confused way, which gives no lead to teachers, under "special interests and maturity".'

2 There is often a lack of space for recording the level of social development and the environmental factors which affect education. As some teachers point out, modern research stresses the effects on children's learning ability of effective socialization and the socio-economic climate which surrounds them but in neither of our specimen record cards is any statement about these factors required.

3 The lack of space for writing about the child's activities in the first school leads teachers too often to make rather unhelpful comments. For example, a typical record card was filled up as follows:

Reading
Very poor reading at first; progressed on ita quite well. (But no indication of exact level reached or the nature of difficulties encountered.)

Language: verbal/written
Jane does not communicate very much. Writing poor, improving gradually. (Again, exact nature of difficulties or level of achievement remains unstated.)

> *Mathematics*
> More capable at this subject. (Does this mean more capable than other children or than at other subjects?) Work is often incomplete. (Why does this pattern continually recur?)

As one head wrote, 'To receive an official LEA card from another school on which a child is labelled "a poor reader" with no further details about the reading scheme used or the book being read is not helpful to the new school. The information on these cards is sometimes so sparse that one wonders, apart from the official requirements, why ever they were sent. If the cards were accompanied by the children's books, they might be more useful. It is the exception rather than the rule to receive books from other schools. Teachers seem to have a deep rooted suspicion about forwarding books which could be so very valuable to another school.'

Many integrated-day teachers would prefer a school record card which allowed space for integrated comments which would give a rounded picture of the individual child. Some suggest that the record card should simply provide a space for each year of the child's infant-school life, in which his teacher can write freely. Others recommend a section for recording 'any family or neighbourhood circumstances that might affect the child's attitudes and ability in school', and also space for writing each year about the child's attitudes towards adults and other children.

On the other hand, some integrated-day teachers find these LEA record cards useful, even in their present form. They recognize that pinpointing each child's development in the basic skills, at a particular point in time, and a careful analysis of his strengths and weaknesses, may be helpful to them as teachers as well as to the child's second school. In the general interest and flow of the integrated day, the teacher can be seduced into enjoyment of a lively, enterprising class and beautifully displayed work without, perhaps, giving sufficient attention to the actual results achieved by a particular child in relation to his potential. This euphoria can be reduced when the teacher is required, at the end of the year, to make exact statements about performance and to place each child within a grade. She may be led to reconsider such difficulties as the meaning of grades and what is meant by the term 'basic skills'.

Teachers are often confused about literal grades, wondering whether grade A or E means very advanced and extremely weak in relation to the rest of this particular class, or in relation to the school record over a number of years, or in relation to some general standard or norm applicable to all children of this age, derived from the use of standardized tests. Where the literal gradings are regarded as a five-point scale with percentage meanings, every class will usually contain some children in every grade, whereas interpretation in relation to a general standard will mean that schools with a rich cultural background and a high socio-economic status will have a large proportion of AS and BS, while EPA schools will have their grades slanting in the opposite direction.

For example, all the children in two seven-year-old classes — one from a culturally advantaged area and one from an EPA area — were tested verbally on the Holborn Language Development scale. Represented graphically, the results were:

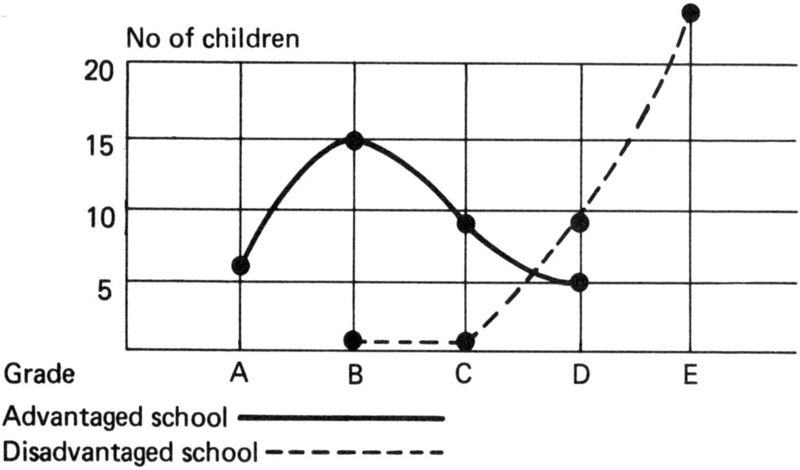

If these grades were to be entered on the record card exactly as achieved they would appear as follows:

	School A	School B
A	6 children	0 children
B	15 children	1 child
C	9 children	1 child
D	5 children	9 children
E	0 children	24 children

But if the per cent system was adopted, in *both* classes, roughly 5 per cent of children would be given the A grade, 15 per cent the

B grade, 60 per cent the C grade, 15 per cent the D grade and 5 per cent the E grade. Of course, with such small numbers (thirty-five in each class) these percentages could not be more than a guide, but the record cards might well have looked like this:

School A

A 6 children
B 9 children (the nine highest BS)
C 15 children (the six lower BS and the CS)
D 4 children
E 1 child (the weakest of the DS)

School B

A 2 children (B and C)
B 9 children (D on the test)
C 15 children (the best of the ES)
D 5 children (the middle ES)
E 4 children (the weakest ES)

It is an arguable point whether second schools find more help in records that use a per cent basis and provide scatter in grading, (indicating that out of a particular class, these five children are the most advanced and those the weakest), or in records based on test results (showing that all the class is advanced or weak in relation to the general school population of the particular age and that special problems are thereby created). Teachers seem to feel that, where grading is obligatory on LEA record forms, some indication of the meaning to be given to the grades should be included on the form.

The choice of skills to be reported on is also a subject of much discussion. Many report forms emphasize the three RS; some also lay emphasis on speech and verbal ability and some ask for information about 'handwork'. Integrated-day teachers often told us that they regarded listening with understanding as a basic skill of equal importance with speech and verbal expression. The importance of assessing the level of reasoning and logic reached by each child is also stressed by many teachers, who feel that this is an indication of future development in many spheres and that the integrated day gives them unrivalled opportunities for seeing how each child sets about solving problems as well as the kind of problems he chooses and the results he achieves. In view of the increasing interest in music both in and out of schools, many teachers would like to have musical ability also considered as 'basic skill'.

Integrated-day teachers, with a wealth of observation to draw on, also find confusion in such terms as 'written English' or 'language — verbal/written. Reporting on such young children, teachers tend to confuse 'handwriting', which is a muscular skill, with 'creative writing', and to write reports such as 'writing poor, improving gradually'. Some teachers suggested that sections for manipulative control and for gross motor control would be helpful.

We found, therefore, that although some integrated-day teachers were not averse to school record cards that sectionalized the items to be recorded, saying that a definite format helped them to clarify their thoughts, all these teachers wanted the categories extended and clarified. Other integrated-day teachers, however, simply wanted blank spaces for each year in which they could write what seemed to them important.

From our discussions with teachers, two positive suggestions emerged, apart from the suggestion that the record cards themselves needed revising. Many integrated-day teachers and some LEA advisors recommend stapling extra pages to the record card, so that a rounded picture of the child can be given. One advisor suggested that each child would need three foolscap pages to hold his first school record. This rounded picture is seen as essential, for teachers realized that reports and ratings only refer to the particular point in time when the report is being written, and are not necessarily prognostic (for example, all children of eight who cannot read are not necessarily dull, nor are all advanced readers necessarily clever). At the time when the report form is being completed, a child may be catching-up on difficulties or living in an unusually favourable situation; unless these factors are recorded an unreal picture will be given, for any child is to some degree a product of his environment.

Moreover, a rounded picture will contain descriptions of special abilities or disabilities. Some disabilities can remain undiscovered for two or three years of a child's school life. For instance, one hears of children whose partial deafness or defective sight remain undiagnosed until they are seven or eight years old by which time the child has become accustomed to thinking of himself as inferior and backward. A rounded report would endeavour to convey to a second school what the handicap has meant in terms of lost opportunity in the first school. On the other hand some special aptitudes, such as musical ability, show themselves early and require careful fostering and special education, as in the case of the ten year old girl, much quoted in the newspapers, described by her music teachers as 'having been born with an oboe in her mouth'. If a suitable standard of early training is not forthcoming, the child's potential may be stultified or ruined by bad habits. As we have stated earlier, integrated-day teachers have unique opportunities for discovering gifted children and need the space on record cards to pass on detailed information to the next school.

The second positive suggestion was that teachers need guidance from their heads about how to make the best use of LEA record cards, in particular how to give exact and factual information and the interpretation to be put on grades where these are required. It was felt that these points should always be discussed between the heads of the first and second schools and an agreed area of required fact and meaningful grading established. In some areas, the use and interpretation of LEA record cards is made, from time to time, the subject of headteachers' meetings and class teachers seemed to find this helpful.

One of the main problems about official record cards seems to arise from a conflict between the amount that integrated-day teachers know about their children and want to record and the amount that second school teachers will read and use. It was felt that very full records should be passed from school to school, in case such information might be needed by psychologists or welfare workers later on, but that teachers in the second school would be unlikely to read a mass of material or find it meaningful. Some teachers suggested that each record should be accompanied by a short précis. Another suggestion was that there should be some way of indicating which children's records need immediate and special attention.

Internal school records

In most schools record cards were also devised by the headteacher and all her staff were required to complete them at stated intervals, so that in a sense these records could also be called 'official'. In some schools and with some types of record they remained within the school, though the information was available for all teachers who needed it, but other schools posted the records to the new head whenever the child transferred. As these records were devised by heads and teachers themselves in integrated schools, they indicate the kinds of record sheets that these teachers are likely to find acceptable. We found six different types of school record with numerous variations on each.

First, *a card index* of essential facts. These cards — one for each child — were usually kept in the secretary's or the head's office. The teachers could consult them when necessary. Most schools keep such cards ready for quick reference in case the child is ill or has an accident, but some of the integrated-day schools had a new section on parental interests and hobbies so that the head or teachers could easily discover how to invite parental cooperation. An example of such a card is given below (the names and dates are fictitious).

Card index reference

JONES, Jane Emma (29.4.67)
5 Crossdale Road, Leicester Tel. 645196
Father John Accountant, Black & Co, Leics 93472 Ex 66
Mother part time hairdresser 'Angela's', High Street (10–2 Mon, Tues, Wed; 9–3 Thurs and Fri) Leics 93759
Country of origin England
Religion C of E
Adopted No
Father's interests sailing, stamp collecting
Mother's interests gardening, painting
(brother in Juniors)

Second, *progress folders* related to the basic syllabus adopted by the school, which underlies the teacher's thinking about and planning for the integrated day. This kind of record is geared to obtaining clear, factual information about each child's interests and work. To complete it satisfactorily, the teacher must reflect, consider and analyse the child's experience and attainments and should be helped to think of him in a definite but rounded way. Such records seemed to be an aid to clear thinking and are also written in a form that could be easily assimilated or referred to by the second school.

Below are three examples of such 'official' progress folders: the first from a school where the children learn to read using ita, later when they are ready transferring to traditional orthography. The other folders are from a school where the children use TO throughout.

Progress folder 1

Farm Lodge Infant School

Name *Age on leaving*

Number work
Sorting grading grouping rearranging a group
matching estimating comparisons
Numbers to 10 — recognition — bonds — subtractions
Numbers to 20 — recognition — bonds — subtractions
Counting with 10s 5s 2s 4s 3s
Knowledge of numbers to 100
Experience of multiplication — division — simple fractions
Practical — measurement — hands — feet — etc
Weight — balancing
Water — capacity
Shape and size
Graphs
Logic blocks
M.A.B.
Money
Time
Symmetry

Writing
Pencil grip correct
Writes own name
Tracing over in crayon or pencil
Copying under teacher's writing
Difficulties
Word building
Writing own news
Writing own stories
Comprehension work
Letter formation — reversals e.g.:
ascenders formed correctly
descenders formed correctly
closed shapes formed

Reading
Right-handed left-handed

Prereading
Knows RH from LH
Speech
Sight
Hearing
Matching
ita characters — sounds — known
Difficulties

Reading Scheme — Parallel Readers
Downing 1 2 3 4 R(a) 5 6 7 8 R(b)
The Monster
Where are Arthur and Helen?
Extension Readers A
Extension Readers B
Extension Readers C
Transfer Series
Difficulties
TO Readers

Creative work

Music

Progress folder 2

The Castle County Infant School

Name *Age on leaving*

Reading
Prereading work: reading readiness books, matching and reading captions, matching word and pictures, matching sentence and pictures, flash cards.
Basic reading scheme: *Janet and John* or *Ladybird*

Stage 1 *Title of book and scheme*

Stage 2

Stage 3

Letter names and single sounds, specify double sounds, word blending.

Stage 4

Stage 5

Stage 6

Double sounds and word endings in detail.

Extension Readers

Penguin and Puffin Readers

Written work
Handwriting: Marion Richardson Writing Patterns. Copying over teacher's writing. Copying under teacher's writing. Letter formation. Spacing.

Creative writing: Writing a simple sentence. Writing several sentences. Writing stories and poems.

Comprehension work: Ladybird Comprehension Cards. Nature Picture Cards. Reading Workshop.
Capable of written work within a centre of interest.
Capable of individual topic work.

Mathematics/concept formation
Dienes Logical Blocks   Stern Structural Apparatus
Experience of sorting, grouping, grading, matching, estimation.
Sealey and Gibbon *Beginning Mathematics*
Book 2 cards   Book 3 cards   Book 4 cards
Junior Number Bond Cards

Environmental mathematics
Shapes   Mapping   Graphs — pictorial
Time: hour, half, quarter, five minutes, 24 hour clock.
Money: matching, recognition of coin to 10 pence, over 10 pence, shopping.
Weight: balancing, weighing to 1 kilo, 500 grams, 250 grams and under 250 grams.

Measurement: feet, hands, digits, spans, paces, strides
to a metre using half metres and decimetres
more than a metre, using centimetres and introducing perimeter, circumference and diameter
Additional practical work attempted.

Creative abilities
Special interests.
Difficulties.

Date	Signature of teacher	(First year)
Date	Signature of teacher	(Second year)
Date	Signature of teacher	(Third year)

Notes for teachers on the keeping of records

Redbridge Infant School

Language development
How does the child converse? Easily, freely or with difficulty? What is the extent of his vocabulary? How good is his use of grammatical structures? Does the child convey ideas through speech? Is his speech clear and distinct or do any letters cause difficulty? Has this developed or diminished since the last notes were made?

Reading
Be very specific here. Did he read easily, or with difficulty? If he had difficulties, what were they? Was there a platform stage, or did he progress easily from one level to the next? Can child sound words and word-build? Does he read for pleasure? Or for information? Does he use the library? Does he read with understanding? The term 'fluent reader' is not sufficient — by whose standards? i.e. now reading. . . .

Written work (including handwriting)
Can child write his own name — or full name? Do writing patterns show control and good formation? Can child copy under, or trace over teacher's writing — either words, captions or phrases? Can he copy from a board? Can he write a sentence, or several sentences about his own pictures, or experiences? Can he write freely, using a wide vocabulary? Can he write a story imaginatively? Or rewrite a story? Can he use a dictionary? Is letter formation good, fair or poor?

Mathematical ability
Be specific. Can the child group and sort? Does he understand notation and the value of numbers — to 10, to 20, to 100 etc? Can he count forward, backwards, singly and in groups? Can he count on, and back in 2s, and 3s etc from any given number? 1–1 correspondence? Does he understand place value? Does he understand the four rules? Does he speak mathematically? What difficulties has he in maths?

Creative interests and manipulative ability
Does child show interest and enjoyment in creative work? Manual dexterity? Which skills has he mastered, e.g. cutting, pasting, modelling, painting, crayoning? Does he use colours well in painting? Does he produce satisfactory results in his work, so that it is pleasing to other people as well as to himself?

Special interests
Has child any hobbies or interests, e.g. scientific or mechanical tendencies? Does he collect stamps, wild flowers, cars? Does he have shared interests with his parents, e.g. camping, fishing etc?

Special difficulties
Wears glasses? Left-handed? (Needs understanding.) Poor sight and hearing? Disturbing behaviour? Inability to concentrate or persevere? Any other problem.

General comments — social development etc
Do *not* put 'a happy well-adjusted child'. This is not clinical enough in a child profile study. Note attitude towards work, other children and adults. Can child adjust and adapt himself? Is he reliable, able to concentrate? Can he lead other children — and in the right way? How is he developing as a person?

Language development

Reading

Written work (including handwriting)

Mathematical ability

Creative interest and manipulative ability

Special interests

Special difficulties

General comments: social development etc

Third, *progress folders* which are not geared to any basic syllabus but are simply a compilation of jottings continued by successive teachers throughout a child's school life. During the first-school life, a picture can be built up in this way which may be very revealing, for example, the record card of Cyril Brown below:

The Tower Infant School

Name Cyril Brown
Adm. April '70, age 5.1 years *Age on leaving*
1st child — St Peter's Playgroup

1970
Withdrawn — says very little. Still rather uncommunicative — immature.
Sept. Very immature — babyish, does not think for himself.
18 Sept. A sudden tremendous effort here in reading — knows all words from Downing 1, 2, 3, 4 books — very enthusiastic — quite a change!
2 Oct. Reading with confidence tackling new words — has learnt *all* his sounds in two weeks — a tremendous effort.
29 Oct. Good progress in reading — writing still very poor.
25 Nov. Remarkable progress with reading. Writing uncoordinated and immature still.

1971
18 Jan. Reading very fluently books a, b, c, now on book d. Writing slightly improved.
29 Jan. Reading very good, now on book d. Poor Cyril finds all recording hard — both in writing and in maths — he is way behind the others in this. Still very immature. Careless with things like clothes after PE etc. I wonder if too much is done for Cyril at home.
12 Feb. Cyril has been away with chicken pox.
12 March Changed to TO with ease, but he is such a baby, he does not know where any of his things are. He has no responsibility for his own things or school things. His reading is excellent but he is too immature to follow assignments involving the most simple reading. Maths — quite poor.
31 March After a talking to, his approach to assignment cards has improved but he still does not use his reading ability to its full

potential. His written work generally has shown improvement recently. He does lack confidence, he never wants to join in any drama or class assembly.
5 May Very immature still — lazy to use reading — written work improving — careless — will not use reading for assignments.
June Poor Cyril is happiest when he is working with a group copying teacher's work or doing more formal things involving precise rules and well used routines. He seems to avoid using initiative, he is such a *little* boy. Writing much improved. Reading very well, he is on to *Pirate Scheme*.
August Still painfully shy — he will not ask when 'stuck'. Spelling very uncertain — writes completely in ita even though he was one of the first onto TO. Reads rapidly, loves to read. I believe Cyril will occasionally wet his pants in school.
November Writing very poor in formation, beginning to improve in content.
6 Dec. Since Cyril had spectacles for long sight he is coping more easily with his written work. He copes fairly well in maths, easily confused — not adventurous in any subject.

1972
13 Jan. Cyril seems a *little* more outgoing just now.
March Cyril benefited by student's visit — he is much more outgoing. Quiet sense of humour. Will accept criticism and teasing. More communicative.
May Trying harder with work. Finishing off more often.
June Parents came to open evening, they are cooperative and interested but quite shy themselves.

This kind of continuous, informal record is most valuable where the information is summarized at intervals and constructive suggestions are made, either by the headteacher or the class teacher or by both. From Cyril Brown's record it might have been deduced by the end of 1970 that his writing difficulties might be due to long sight (which might not really affect his reading since he could alter the position of the book in a way impossible for writing) or to slight spasticity. In June 1972 the parents' attitude suggests that Cyril's shyness may be partly learned from them and would respond to social encouragement and reeducation as noted in March 1972. There is also a possibility that his pleasure and skill in reading is connected with a desire to escape into a safe but interesting world, free from social demands. Teachers who use this form of record find that time spent in reflecting on their observations is often very rewarding and may well suggest points to be taken up with the headmistress, the parents or the school doctor.

Fourth, *record sheets* based on the normal developmental sequences of various abilities. These are compiled, not on the school syllabus as in progress folders 2A and 2B (pp. 171–4), but from a combination of the teachers' own experiences together with their reading about research into child development or enquiries into the learning, teaching or development of particular skills. An example of such a record used for the skill of reading by the teachers of Commonmead School is given here. This record sheet is quickly filled up, the teachers only having to tick the items for which a positive score is given. This kind of record is also very easily read by the second school and therefore likely to be really used by teachers to whom it is sent. It does not, however, record the actual reading scheme in use nor the book on which the child is working though it could easily be made to do so.

Commonmead School

Name:	*1st Year*	*2nd Year*	*3rd Year*
A Child's attitude to reading			
Interested			
Happy and relaxed			
Willing to do his best			
Very attentive			
Able to carry out work without requesting unnecessary help			
Independent and confident			
B Child's reading habits			
Good left to right eye movements			
Makes big eye sweeps			
Regressive eye movements			
Finds place and keeps it			
Guesses at random			
Omits or substitutes words			
Reads along in natural easy manner			
Observes punctuation			

C Child's skill in word perception

Recognizes sight words readily
Tends to confuse similar words
Remembers unusual new words
Recognizes likeness and differences in word forms
Blends letters into words
Is helpless before new words
Knows letter sounds
Can say alphabet
Can tackle some words independently

D Child's ability to interpret what he reads

Understands what he has read
Anticipates what is coming next in the text
Recalls events in proper sequence
Can answer questions about the text
Can interpret the pictures from the text
Can carry out assignments of work on his reading
Can use reading for different purposes
  recreation
  problem solving
  information
  entertainment of others

Fifth, *a record folder* for each child into which was stuck, at the end of each term, an example of the child's work in handwriting, creative writing, mathematics and art. In some schools children are encouraged to choose the examples and stick them into the folder for themselves, as soon as they become capable of such selection, and they usually derive great pleasure in looking back through their folders to note their own increased skill and progress towards the longed-for state of being 'grown-up'. These folders are usually very interesting to parents when they visit the school and are a simple, factual way of showing them what their child is actually achieving. One or two schools include a large envelope in each folder into which are put letters from the child's parents and his medical records. In these schools, children are not allowed access to the record folders but there is the advantage that all information is available for reference under one cover.

Sixth, *a profile* of each child's development is kept in some schools. This is based on a number of developmental and learning items worked out by the teachers and written in a vertical column. There is one typed sheet provided for each child. For each separate item, the child is rated each year on a five-point scale and the rating is indicated by a dot placed at the appropriate point. The dots are then joined with a particular coloured biro for the year, and the child's educational profile can be seen. An example of this method might be as follows (first year indicated by unbroken line):

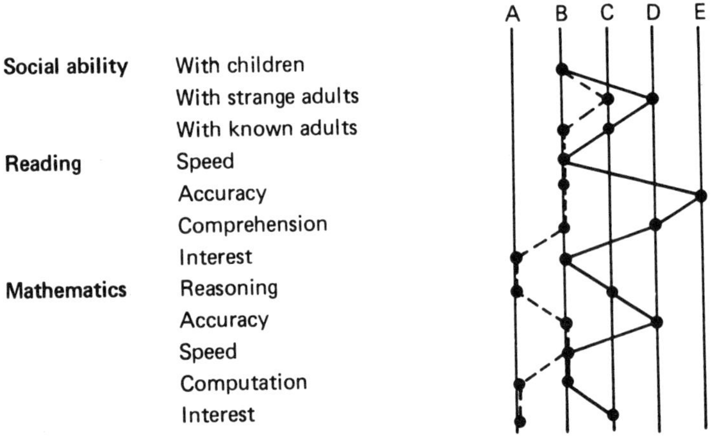

This profile, to which many other items would normally be added, shows at a glance a very middle-of-the-road child. But in the second year (indicated by a broken line) the picture changes. One can see at a glance that he has become more socially adapted to adults and more interested in his school work. He shows a developing mathematical ability which his third year profile may reveal has developed further while, on the other hand, his next profile may show that some other interest and skill has overtaken it. These educational profiles, if the items are carefully chosen, does give at a glance a very telling record of the child's changing development.

These are the six main kinds of school record that we have seen, though every type varies from school to school according to the experience and needs of the particular teachers and pupils, and their relationship with the second school that follows.

Teachers' own records

In addition to the official records required by the LEA and the semiofficial records required by most headteachers, most class teachers working an integrated day kept their own records in their own way for their personal satisfaction. These records we found particularly interesting since almost every teacher had her own way of recording and some of the methods were very ingenious. Apart from individual variations, however, we found that teachers own records in general belonged to one of four categories.

Records that itemise progress

Reading records

Most teachers keep reading records of some kind, usually showing the days when individual children have read to the teacher, together with the book and page last read. Teachers who are using a basic reading scheme quite often record on cards, which they keep handy in the children's reading books, writing on them the date and page each time they hear a child read. This is the simplest, basic form of record but it does not give the teacher any view of class progress as a whole or any means of noting a child's particular interests or weaknesses. Some teachers, therefore, let each child make a small notebook into which they can enter such details when they hear him read, together with words or sounds not known. Other teachers write reading assignments where needed in these notebooks. In order to keep an overall picture of the class's reading progress, some kind of graphical record is commonly made. In some classes, teachers make a vertical list of their pupils on the left hand side of a page which is then ruled into columns, each column being headed with a date. Often this kind of record is kept by the month.

Date	May 1	2	3	4	5	8	9	10	11	12	15	16	17
Name													
Justin Archer													
Margaret Austin													
Mandy Barnes													
Sarah Cann													
Paul Cartwright													
etc.													

These columns are sometimes merely ticked when a child reads to the teacher, but other teachers write the page and an abbreviated symbol for the book the child is reading which gives some picture of how each child is progressing in relation to the class. One teacher used a different colour for each day of the week, while others used a different colour for each book in a series of readers and we found that colour certainly made the record easier to interpret. In some classes, the teacher made a separate record of this type for each book in the series and as a child began a new book, his name was added to the vertical column for that book. This gave teachers a very clear idea of the speed of each child's advance. They were also able clearly to see the length of time that children with reading difficulties were spending on one book and perhaps gain an added insight into the depths of their boredom.

Comprehensive records

In addition to reading records, some teachers kept more comprehensive records including mathematics records, handwriting records and creative writing records while a few teachers kept a record of particularly interesting art and creative activities. Some teachers recorded almost every aspect of their work saying that over the years it helped to build up a reference library to which they could refer again and again. One of these complete records, kept fortnightly, is as follows:

June 6th–June 15th

Stories Seven at one blow, Little John Little, Four Friends of Bremen, Boy who ran away.

Poems 'Tea time', 'The dandelion', 'The five flowers'

Assembly 'Summer has come' — talk about summer flowers, trees, grasses, fields and gardens.

Music Heehaw. Dandelion clocks. Summer has come. (Songs)

Creative work Group making a flower picture with materials. Making papier mâché picnic plates. Children went on a walk through the village on Wednesday afternoon to look at flowers and gardens. Through various media they interpreted what they had seen. Border patterns round creative writing.

Another example of a comprehensive record is given on p. 183.

In schools where teachers have access to duplicators of some kind a teacher may analyse the various skills to be expected in her class, duplicate a form for each child and enter a tick or the date when the skill is first observed. One such teacher, in a school with a high proportion of immigrants, made the record sheet on p. 184.

Name	Main interest	Reading	Maths experience	Writing	Observation
Kim Antill	Painting people and flowers in village gardens. Mathematics.	*Bk4* 19, 27. Finished *Bk5*.	100 squares. Work with shapes for flower picture.	Makes b d backwards. Writing about shapes.	Seems more interested in reading lately.
Carol Ball	Creative writing. Poem about summer. Border patterns.	*Bk6* 40, 46, 48. Read *Bk7* at home.	Making numbers to 20.	Own story and poem. Concertina book *Summer*.	Rather solitary child but seems happy. Watch this.
Simon Deane	Papier mâché plate, painted decoration.	*Bk3* 6, 7, 8.	Making cakes, weighing in 250 gms. Recording.	Group book about the cakes we made.	Since parents evening has concentrated more.
Deborah Fisher	Reading poems. Flower picture with materials.	*It Must be Magic* 72, 84, 90.	Work with shapes for flower picture.	Own story 'About a ladybird'.	Brings interesting items of news.
Sarah Eaton	Sewing, embroidered flower picture. Reading.	*High on the Hill* 25, 33, 55, 76.	Work with shapes for flower picture.	Writing about shapes. Makes a wrongly — correct this.	Difficult to teach her sewing as she is left-handed. Practise myself.

Language skills   *Date*

Name

Understands but does not speak English
Speaks English in disjointed words
Speaks English in phrases or sentences
Sings rhymes and songs
Speaks English clearly and fluently
Shows power of concentration
Contributes to class discussions
Shows understanding of stories, wall stories, poems and oral work
Hears sounds in word games
Interprets pictures:
  verbally
  into writing
Compares and matches pictures, shapes, objects, words
Draws freely and discusses what he has drawn
Can form letters
Has good control of writing tools
Traces accurately
Copies labels on own drawings
Records own experiences with help
Can read own records
Can read room notices
Recognizes words in different context
Reads phrases and writes them
Attempts creative writing:
  with visual aid
  without visual aid
Writes freely
Uses library books:
  Looks at pictures
  Reads stories
  Uses for information
Uses word books
Uses capital letters correctly generally
Punctuation
Compiles and uses own dictionary
Can comprehend library books in class
  simple
  average
  difficult

Seeks information in books and uses it purposefully
Can create own stories, write and illustrate them

Jotting

Teachers may use other ways of recording as well as the rather stereotyped records we have so far discussed or they may use informal types of records only. Most teachers who keep informal records base them on what are commonly called 'jottings'. Teachers organize themselves to jot on a variety of materials, the main point being that the jotter shall be easily available all the time. The aim is to keep an on-the-spot record of the children's more important activities, learnings or sayings which indicate their level of thought and comprehension and their social awareness. Teachers also jot down reminders to themselves as the occasion occurs. Some teachers jot on cards carried in the pocket or kept in an open box in some suitable place while others use a pad, often kept on the teacher's table. One teacher clipped a sheet of paper to a board, hung it up and wrote in shorthand while one or two relied on the illegibility of their handwriting and the fact that young children can hardly read even well-written 'double-writing', and did the same thing. At the end of the day, these jottings were entered up, either in the teacher's daily diary (which formed the basis for her work plan for the next day), or on the child's own page in her record book. The advantages in keeping such a book are that it draws the teacher's attention to the children towards whom she is directing too much observation, as their pages quickly become full, at the expense of those whom she is rather neglecting, as their pages remain empty. Jotting, maintained over a long period, really helps to build up a lively, rounded view of each child in a way that the more stereotyped forms of recording do not. On the other hand, jottings may give a picture of the living child without accurate information about his skills. Probably both methods should be used in conjunction.

Flow charts

Another common form of record is the flow chart, which is also used by teachers for planning ahead. We have dealt with flow charts earlier (pp. 104–6), but we found one school which had a particularly ingenious way of keeping the chart handy. The class had a double, sliding wall blackboard and the flow chart, written on the underneath board, was preserved by sliding the top board over it when the chart was not in use. As it was always available, the teacher could consult the chart, refer back to work done, alter it and add to it on the spot. Teachers can encourage the oldest children in a first school to build-up their own group flow chart to record the work done and remind them of what they have decided about future work.

In many classrooms we saw these charts on the wall but a more practical form of chart (it is easily altered or rearranged and costs nothing to make) is the flannel graph. A piece of heavy cardboard such as an old show card, is covered with a piece of woollen, plain material cut from an old skirt, vest etc, or a coloured duster. The items of the flow chart are written on pieces of good quality cartridge paper (rectangles 40 × 80 mm are suitable). Woollen fabric is pasted on the back of the paper which will then stick to the flannel graph without an adhesive and can be taken off or moved around as required. The flannel graph can be propped against a wall, a stand can be made from stripwood, while many show cards have their own cardboard supports. Just how useful

Flow chart 1

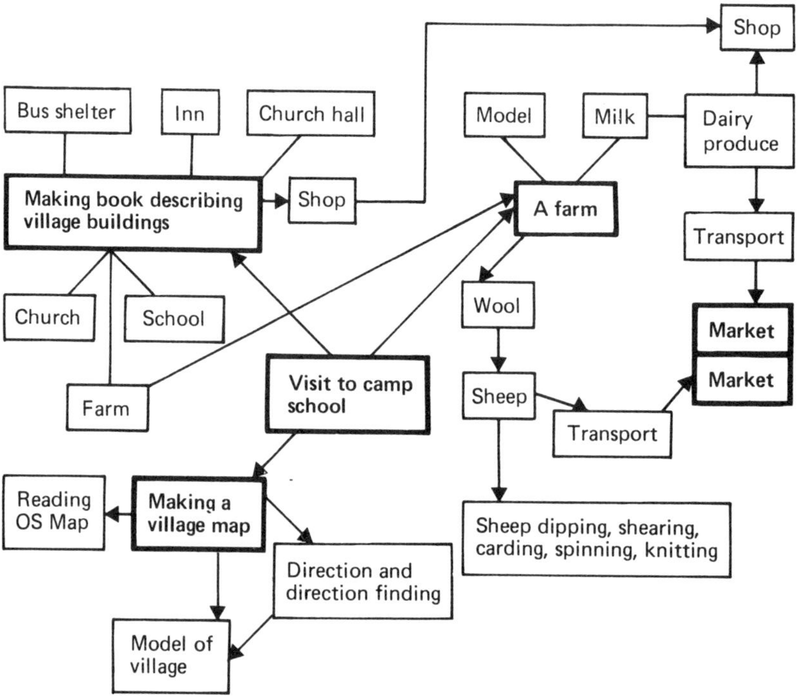

it is to be able to rearrange a flow chart as the work develops can be illustrated by a chart which resulted from a visit by a class of seven to eight year olds to a residential camp school. The children divided into groups to work in various areas. The original chart is on page 186. As the various interests developed, the groups began to use one another's work for information and reference. Sometimes, as with the market, several groups could be working on the same topic and new groupings would form, so that the flow chart would look like this:

Flow chart 2

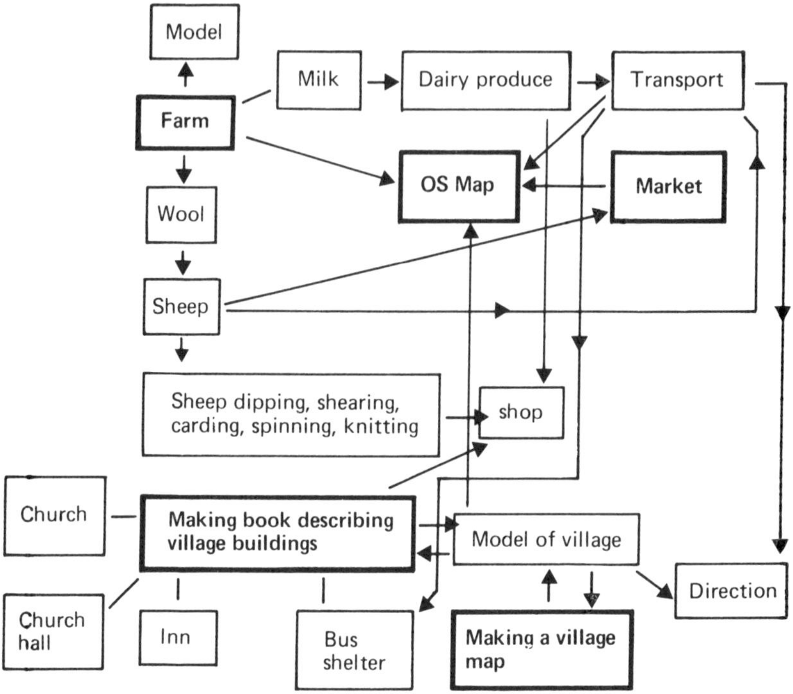

This diagram would help the teacher to see clearly the crucial part played by the ordnance survey map of the village and surrounding country and the way in which many of the original areas or interests converged on transport and the market. It became obvious that a visit to the local market would be needed to develop the ideas of this group of children. Flow charts that can be rearranged and altered are very helpful to the teacher in integrating and realigning her ideas.

Folders

Some teachers keep for their own use a folder for each child into which a piece of handwriting, creative writing, mathematics and art are fastened each term. This gives a guide as to the rate and extent of each child's progress.

There are almost as many variations on these six main types of individual record as there are individual teachers to keep them. The actual amount of recording done was described for us by three teachers.

Teacher 1 Mrs Murray

1 Each child started an envelope when he/she began school. In it was put
paintings: to show development (both artistic and emotional in some cases);
important pieces of writing to show: imagination, development in actual writing skill, points the teacher thought relevant to child.

2 I also kept weekly record of work, in note form, showing what interests had developed in the class and each child's part in them.

3 Children's personal development records were kept in separate book. We listed anything relevant to the child's development — illness, school medical results, parents' visits on open nights etc, speech therapist's reports.

Teacher 2 Mrs Bell

I always designed and made my own record folders.

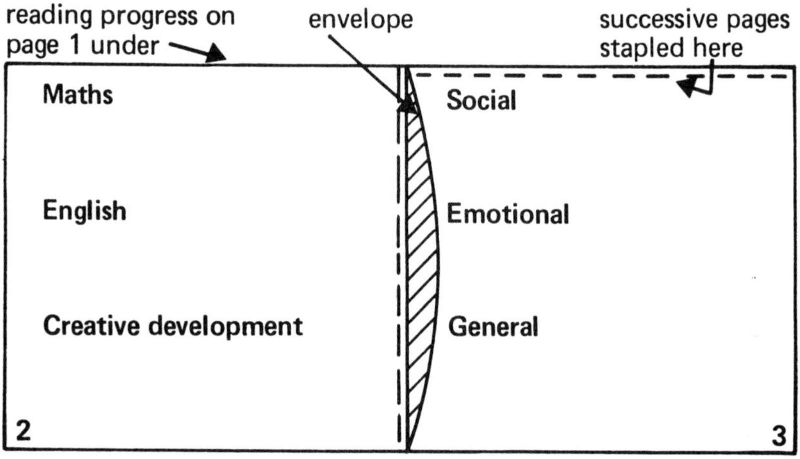

1 On front of record card I recorded reading progress.
2 On second page maths, English, creative development.
3 Envelope was stuck on page 3 for medical reports, letters from parents etc.
4 On a third page, stuck on to the envelope, there was a big space for emotional development, social development, and a general report i.e. attitudes to school, parents' attitude to school and teacher etc.

Teacher 3 Miss Simmons (working in a three-teacher country school)

I always kept these records:

A class record

1 An exercise book lined and named as for an attendance register. Headings were made for individual pieces of work, cards, books, steps in mathematics etc. Items were then 'ticked' as the child finished the work, or as the teacher marked the books.
2 Record cards: a card for each child divided into sections for English, mathematics and reading. I recorded stages completed, books read, cards finished etc.
3 Rest of pages devoted to record:
   Reading Scheme — book — next page to be read.
   Mathematics Sets of numbers learnt — 10–20; stages in time, weight measuring and capacity; money; practical work; Stern; Dienes.
   English Books; cards or sets etc recorded; phonic sounds; comprehension cards.

I have used this method for about eighteen years and find it works very well. It is especially useful when the class teacher is absent as any relief teacher quickly sees the working pattern of each child.

Although all the teachers said that these individual records were never seen by the head, they themselves valued them and felt them to be a most important part of working in an integrated day. It was quite remarkable what a lot of careful, accurate recording was being done and how much teachers could tell about individual children when information was asked for.

Children's own records

In some schools children were taught from the beginning to make some record of each day's work, partly to help the teacher see the day through the children's eyes and partly to focus the attention of the children for a short time each day on what they had been doing. Every parent and teacher knows children who, when asked what they have been doing at school reply, 'nothing', or 'Playing' or 'I don't know'. This may be a defensive measure but it may equally be inertia, lack of words or lack of thought and a simple record helps overcome the latter difficulties without violating the defences too much. Further, it is often very instructive for teachers to see the difference between their view of the child's day and the child's. The teacher may think that John has been reading but the significant experience for John was finding a dead slow worm in the school playground and the questions he asked about it.

In general we found five main types of record with many variations on each.

First type

With very young children, the record usually consisted of some form of wall chart, with a heading such as 'Today I have used' and the children's names written down the left-hand side. These charts are filled up in different ways according to the children's ability. Young children are often asked to colour in squares according to a key or to choose a square or star of coloured paper and stick it by their name, for example Wendy house may be blue, painting red etc. This may be done at the end of the day in group discussion. Alternatively a piece of pegboard can be used with pictures or names of the activity along the top and pegs inserted below on which children can hang name cards. Other varieties develop where children can read a little. Either a list of names can be written and an old envelope stuck to the side of each, into which the child puts a card with the name of the activity, selected from a pile written previously by the teacher, or a column of envelopes or pockets is prepared by the teacher for each activity and the children put their name cards in the appropriate pocket. Older or more competent children simply sign their names or write the name of the activity. If a strip of paper is used for the writing, it can be changed each day.

Some teachers vary their records. Children can be encouraged to think about such experiences as 'Today I listened to', (my teacher, my friend, a bird, the wind, the watertap, music, people's feet etc) or 'Today I made', (a new sum, a story, a picture, a dance etc).

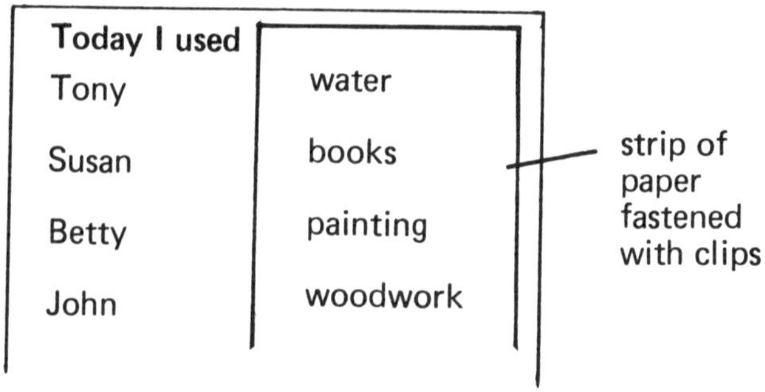

There seem to be two important points about these records: they should not make children competitive and every child should be able to record something positive. Teachers therefore seemed to find it advisable to ask the children to record only the one most important or interesting thing each day and even the slowest, most diffident, most backward child will have one thing to enter, while the quickest, liveliest child can be taught to select the best so that they all end with one entry each day. They also leave the record on view for one day only, changing the record paper or cards each afternoon, so that children engaged in repeating an activity day after day do not build up a picture of themselves for other children to see and remark 'He always plays with the water'. The record is to help the individual child and the teacher to realize his potential; it is not intended for general class criticism. However, teachers say that they are often asked for extra labels (e.g. looked at the tadpoles) and usually keep a set of spare cards for this.

Second type

The oldest children in some schools are asked to make a notebook in which they keep a short diary of what they have done, usually writing it up towards the end of the afternoon, e.g. 'Read Chapter 2. Wrote book about Magic Roundabout. Made a sputnik.' These record diaries may be seen by the teacher at stated intervals. Their purpose is to make the child aware of how he has used his day.

Third type

In a few schools we found that teachers had made wall-pockets or used commercially-produced plastic slipper-pockets, with a pocket for each child with his name clearly marked. Inside each pocket was a card on which the teacher entered anything that she particularly wished the child to do or practise. These assignments were sometimes entered during the day, while she was talking to the child, and sometimes as part of her preparation at home while she was reflecting on the day's observations or classifying her jottings. Each day children would refer to their cards to see if there were special assignments for them. When a child had completed his assignment, he would put a tick and show the work to the teacher. Not all children would have assignments every day, only those for whom the teacher felt some particular work would be helpful.

Fourth type
A few teachers told us that they kept separate books for recording work in reading, mathematics, creative writing, art, constructive work etc, which children signed when they had completed work in a particular area or else put a tick by their names. This method of recording was found particularly useful for those engaged in team teaching as it helped teachers and children to see that, over a period of time, their work was not becoming unbalanced with undue emphasis on one form of learning only.

Fifth type
We have already mentioned (page 179) the type of record where actual specimens of work done by the children are stuck into progress folders. In certain schools, these folders are the property of the children. Each child will choose a piece of work from each activity area to stick into his own book each term so that, as the term progresses, a teacher may say to a child, 'Isn't that interesting?' or 'Well done' or 'Would you like it for your progress book?' leaving it to the child to agree or not. Children enjoy these record books. It fascinates them to be able to refer back, see themselves growing away from 'baby' work and note their own increase in power, knowledge and skill.

On the whole, it was a minority of first schools where the children themselves kept records but when this was done, the teachers seemed to feel that it was valuable and that the children enjoyed it.

Records of standardized test results
Another kind of record used by nearly all schools was some form of standardized test, particularly in reading, for children who

would be progressing to the second school at the end of the current year. Heads thought that these tests were particularly valuable since the standard of each child could be roughly ascertained, not merely in relation to other children in the particular school, but in relation to all children in all other normal schools. It is thus possible for any head to see whether the reading ability of any child or group of children is above or below the average standard for the age in the total school population.

Many schools seem to use the Schonell *Graded Reading Vocabulary Test* which helps a headteacher to arrive quickly and simply at a 'reading age' for the recognition of words out of context. Where the test is given at intervals to children who present reading problems, the cumulative records can help teachers to see whether slow readers are making progress in this skill or whether accelerated readers are still using material incommensurate with their powers. Appropriate steps can then be considered in the light of these records.

Other schools use the full battery of Schonell tests which include also *Prose Reading Tests* and *Silent Reading Tests* and, where difficulties are found, a set of *Diagnostic Tests*, on which remedial work can be based. Since all this demands time and a quiet place, tests are usually administered by the headteacher and we found that the full range of tests are only used with children who present special difficulties, either because they are particularly advanced or retarded. Test records were sometimes passed to the teachers and sometimes not, but heads in general discussed the child's reading record with the teacher concerned and helped her, if necessary, to make a plan of action. Another test used in the same way in a number of schools is *The Standard Test of Reading* by Daniels and Diack.

A test used by some schools, though perhaps not used enough, is the *Neale Analysis of Reading Ability.* This test enables the tester to analyse out four factors in a child's reading: rate/fluency; accuracy and kinds of errors made; comprehension; emotional attitude to reading. The test material is straightforward for the child, since only one passage has to be read, but the scoring makes demands on the teacher's accuracy and concentration, and a fair amount of practice is required before real testing can be regarded as satisfactory. Records of a child's performance in this test are particularly useful to the teacher since scores on the three factors actually tested are usually unequal and the record clearly indicates the kind of programme that a child needs at a particular time.

In addition to standardized reading tests, which were the tests most commonly used, we found that a few schools gave the children standardized vocabulary tests, the resulting records being related to the reading test records with some very useful results. Since the 'new maths' was introduced into schools, we have found no cases where standardized tests of mathematics are used in infant or first schools.

A record sheet for standardized test results, as used in one school, is given below. This record is completed for each child. The results are discussed with the class teacher in the year in which the test is given and remedial work is arranged if necessary.

Burkwood County Infant School

5–6 yrs

Name *Date of birth*

The Crichton Vocabulary Test Set 1 Set 2 Total

Grade

6–7 yrs

No 2 *The Standard Test of Reading* Daniels and Diack

Age Date Class

Score Reading age Reading standard

Indication of difficulties

Supplementary Tests given:

7–8 yrs

No 3 *Neale Analysis of Reading Ability*

Age Date Class

		Rate/fluency			*Accuracy*	
No. of words in passage	*Passage*	*Words read*	*Time in seconds*	*Errors*	*Accuracy score*	*Comprehension*
26	1					
49(75)	2					
72(147)	3					
92(239)	4					
118(357)	5					
139(496)	6					
	Totals					
Reading Ages						

Ceiling reached for speed, accuracy and comprehension

$$\text{Rate} = \text{words per minute} = \frac{\text{words} \times 60}{\text{time (secs)}} = \frac{\quad}{\quad} = \text{words per minute}$$

This can be drawn without the rate/fluency columns, if this information is not required. Rate/fluency is the most complicated to score as it cannot be tabulated in the instruction book and must be worked out individually for each child.

Teachers seem to feel that standardized test records are valuable only where they are not used as absolute standards, but are considered as helping in the planning of programmes suitable for a particular kind of school or for individual children.

Records using recording equipment

The records that we have so far considered have been concerned mainly with the individual child's work and progress, although some consideration has been given to records of group projects when these are recorded by the teacher in the course of her work. Many schools, however, record the way in which children actually work on projects and also the finished material or display by means of photographs or slides. These are often mounted with explanatory captions or in a booklet compiled by children and teacher, and then put in the school library for reference. If a project book has been compiled by the children, this is also included. In this way, a school can build up its own interesting collection of reference material, which helps to form a sense of continuity and tradition even in rather new schools and can be used to help inexperienced teachers or newcomers to the staff. On open days or parents' evenings, parents have been found to enjoy this kind of pictorial record of work done earlier in the year or when their children first entered school, three years before.

In the same way, tape recorders are used in many schools to record many forms of activity and a library of tapes is gradually built up. The most obvious form of record is where children describe their displays and projects so that, as well as looking at the work, visitors can actually hear the children talking about it. Other uses of tape recorders are making records of the music, stories or poems that children write, recording gifted story tellers or singers — either children or teachers — and recording group events such as bands, simple operas or plays. In this way, a child who has something special to offer the others or a group that has done a worthwhile production can have the pleasure of hearing themselves as well as knowing that their work will last for a long time.

Some of the schools we visited worked closely with the local college of education, which had closed-circuit television and often asked schools to bring children to the studio so that various aspects of work could be recorded. These are then played back to the children and teachers. The children enjoy being TV personalities and feeling that their work is sufficiently valued to appear on the screen, while teachers often get valuable sidelights on the behaviour of the children and their own ways of teaching. In addition, records of this kind are extremely helpful in training students. Some of the TV projects undertaken included a series on play with various kinds of materials, showing how children react at various stages when playing freely with sand, water, building blocks, paint etc, another series on school assemblies, and demonstrations by teachers of hearing and correcting the individual reading of children at various levels. The college has also made a number of TV 'shorts' on teaching reading by various techniques such as ita, Reading in Colour and phonics. There have also been records of children working on various interests and projects. If these are 'put in the can' to be stored, they form excellent material for discussion groups of parents, teachers or visitors. The use of closed-circuit television is still in its infancy in many areas. There is much work to be done before schools and colleges make the most of this equipment and are able to cooperate in the most imaginative, inventive ways to educate teachers, parents and students through visual recording.

Records for parents

In the previous sections we have several times referred to records which are kept mainly by the school for its own use but which can also be used to interest and educate parents. However, we have found certain records that are devised mainly for the parents. The first of these is the school report. Reports seem mainly to have been discontinued in the infant or first school. The modern tendency is to make parents welcome whenever they visit the school, to devise ways of bringing parents into the school community and to rely on face-to-face interviews to keep parents informed about their children. However some parents, for a variety of reasons, never visit the school. In order to make another type of approach to these parents, as well as increasing the chances of two-way communication with all parents, we found that some schools favour sending termly or yearly reports to which parents are asked to reply in a space provided, making their own comments on what the teachers have said. Schools that use this way of recording what the child does and the parents think, find that much useful information is contributed by parents which helps the teacher to a clearer understanding of a child's problems, home circumstances and interests. Heads told us that there were very few parents who, after a term or two, would not cooperate in this scheme, even if they could not or would not visit the school.

We also found that some schools, through the PTA, ran a termly magazine for parents to which both the school staff and the parents contributed. The head was able to use this to tell parents about any schemes or new methods that he had in mind, items of interest in the life of the school, dates of outings, parties and meetings, requests for assistance and information. The parents send in items of general interest such as comments on the head's reports, information on such matters as clothing, films, books and library facilities, reports and financial statements about the PTA. In other schools a broadsheet from the head and her staff is duplicated and sent home to the parents, either at stated intervals or when the head has something of particular interest to record.

The general impression that we gained was that teachers felt that records and recording were of the first importance in the integrated day but that records should be brief, simple and straightforward or they would not be used. Where lengthy records are kept, it was felt that a précis should also be available for immediate reference. For while the actual keeping of a record helps to clarify the teacher's mind and forms an important link between teacher, child and head, it is only when these records are really used as a basis for consultation and planning that they can be said fully to justify the amount of time spent in keeping them.

BIBLIOGRAPHY

CENTRAL ADVISORY COUNCIL FOR EDUCATION (1967) *Children and Their Primary Schools* (Plowden Report) London: HMSO

DES (1972) *Open Plan Primary Schools* (Education Survey No. 16) London: HMSO

HERTZBERG, A. and STONE, E. F. (1971) *Schools are for Children* New York: Schoken Books

RANCE, P. (1971) *Record Keeping in the Progressive Primary School* London: Ward Lock Educational

RINTOUL, K. and THORNE, K. (1975) *Open Plan Organization in the Primary School* London: Ward Lock Educational

WALTON, J. (1971) *The Integrated Day in Theory and Practice* London: Ward Lock Educational

INDEX

Extending and Developing Portage